Ken Garland

ILLUSTRATED GRAPHICS GLOSSARY

of terms used in printing, publishing, photography and other fields
of interest to graphic designers, their clients and their suppliers

Barrie & Jenkins

London   Melbourne   Sydney   Auckland   Johannesburg

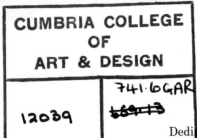
Dedicated to Jesse Collins, Anthony Froshaug and Nigel Henderson:
better teachers than this student ever deserved

and with thanks
to my colleagues and students in the Department of Typography
and Graphic Communication, University of Reading, and the
Department of Graphic Information, School of Graphic Arts, Royal
College of Art, for putting up with my obsessive questions so
helpfully and good-naturedly; to Harriet Crowder, for contributing
many of the photographs; to my wife, Wanda, for coping so well
with the tetchiness attendant on too much burning of midnight oil;
to my associates, Colin Bailey and Peter Cole, for their skilful
collaboration in the preparation of illustrations and layouts; and
most of all, to Richard Southall and to Allen Hurlburt, for their
separate but equally assiduous readings of my manuscript, their
tactful corrections and amendments which have saved me much
embarrassment and their more than welcome suggestions for
additional entries.

First published 1980
© Ken Garland 1980
Published in London by Barrie & Jenkins
3 Fitzroy Square, W1

Designed by Ken Garland and Associates
Typeset by Input Typesetting Ltd in 9/11pt Linotron Century
Printed in Great Britain by
The Anchor Press, Tiptree, Essex

ISBN 0 09 141511 X

Contents

Introduction

This book is intended as a successor to the earlier *Graphics hand-book** and incorporates some lessons drawn from user comments on that publication. It seems that, whilst it was reasonably success-ful as an introduction to the subject in general and to a number of related topics – its primary purpose – it fell short to some extent as a work of rapid reference, partly because of omissions but mainly because, having neither index nor glossary, it was difficult for the reader to know where to look for some particular piece of inform-ation or to know the precise meaning of the more technical terms.

Now, the missing tail has become the dog, as it were, and the book is all glossary. Properly, a glossary is not merely a list of definitions of terms but is also concerned with *explanations*. That is the reason for the many illustrations and for the length of certain of the entries which need more elucidation than straight definitions could provide.

Devising a glossary for an activity so diverse as graphic design is a bit like trying to record every feature in a vast landscape seen from a mountain top: where do you draw the line? I've gone fairly extensively into those terms a designer would expect to encounter in print production, photography and publishing, of course; but what about the less immediate features in the landscape such as film animation, audio-visual aids or electronic data processing and, still more removed, information theory, perceptual psychology or geographical projections? Well, the temptation proved irresistible and so you will find entries here for 'dope sheet', 'epidiascope' or 'drum plotter', also for 'semiotic', 'gestalt' or 'zenithal projections', and many others equally distant from the home territory of the drawing board.

The reasons for including items from such far-flung fields are: firstly, the author has encountered all of them during the course of his work as a graphic designer and would like to spare his readers some of the embarrassment he experienced when confronted with an unknown term he was expected to be conversant with; and

Graphics handbook Studio Vista, 1966, now out of print.

6

secondly, readers may, by picking up a new term from an unfamiliar area, be able to plug in to a new and rewarding area of interest. Anyone who has ever sat down and thumbed through an encyclopaedia with no other aim apart from pure curiosity will know what I mean.

The selection of terms for inclusion was made with great care and with the benefit of much good advice from colleagues, but there may well be gaps; readers are invited – urged – to write to me, care of the publisher, and let me know of any missing terms they would like to see included in any new edition.

There are certain differences in usage between UK and US terms which may on occasion cause confusion; some of these are listed below

UK	US
artwork	mechanical
author's correction	AA (author's alteration)
bevel (of type)	beard
block	cut
blocking	stamping, tooling
caption	cutline, caption
client's rough/visual	comp (comprehensive)
clump (spacing matter)	slug
comp, compositor	typographer, compositor
concertina fold	accordion fold
cutting copy (cinefilm)	workprint
dope sheet (cinefilm)	exposure sheet
em (if not qualified)	pica
end matter (of book)	back matter
full point	period
ink duct	fountain
interleaving	slipsheeting
keyline	holding line
keys (film animation)	extremes
landscape format	horizontal format
lay (of printing press)	guide
literal	typo (typographic error)
machine minder	pressman

mean line	x-line, mean line
mechanical pulp	groundwood pulp
mix (cinefilm)	dissolve
paperback	pocketbook, paperback
pie	pi
prelims (of book)	front matter
presentation visual	comp (comprehensive)
rostrum (film animation)	animation stand
rostrum table	compound table
run on (proof correction)	run in
scraperboard	scratchboard
show print (cinefilm)	release print
slab-serif	square-serif
sloped roman	oblique roman
special sort	pi character
sub-editor	copyreader
s/o (substance of) . . .	base weight . . .
tail, foot	foot
tracking (cinefilm)	trucking
trim marks	crop marks
turn to . . .	jump to . . .
type scale	line gauge
typographer	typographic designer
squared-up halftone	square halftone
stripping-up as one	double-burning, surprinting
woodfree	freesheet

Note: the sign # or 'hache mark', which in UK is used exclusively in type mark-ups and proof corrections to mean 'space', exists in US type founts for use as 'number' or 'item' in listing.

A

AA	initials of 'author's alteration': indication on proof that cost of type correction is author's or publisher's responsibility (used in US but not common in UK)
A and B roll assembly	in cinefilm editing, using two rolls of film instead of one master, each roll containing alternate shots; this facilitates 'fades', 'dissolves' (qqv) and special optical effects
A, B and C series of paper sizes	triple range of paper sizes originally established as 'DIN' standards (qv), then adopted by International Standards Organization (ISO), of which 'A' Series is intended for all kinds of stationery and printed matter, 'B' Series as intermediate alternatives and 'C' Series for envelopes; all sizes are as trimmed or made up and are given in millimetres:

A0 1189 × 841	B0 1414 × 1000	C0 1297 × 917
A1 841 × 594	B1 1000 × 707	C1 917 × 648
A2 594 × 420	B2 707 × 500	C2 648 × 458
A3 420 × 297	B3 500 × 353	C3 458 × 324
A4 297 × 210	B4 353 × 250	C4 324 × 229
A5 210 × 148	B5 250 × 176	C5 229 × 162
A6 148 × 105	B6 176 × 125	C6 162 × 114
A7 105 × 74	B7 125 × 88	C7. 114 × 81
A8 74 × 52	B8 88 × 62	specials:
A9 52 × 37	B9 64 × 44	DL 220 × 110
A10 37 × 26	B10 44 × 31	C7/6 162 × 81

all sizes are proportionate reductions of basic 0 sheet, sides being in ratio $1 : \sqrt{2}$ (1 : 1.4142):

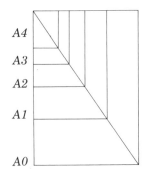
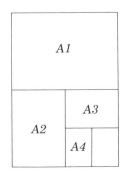

A0 = one square metre
untrimmed sheet size for unbled work: RA0 1220 × 860mm
untrimmed sheet size for bled work: SRA0 1280 × 900mm
DL envelopes are specially intended to accommodate A4 sheets
folded twice to $\frac{1}{3}$A4

above the fold   newspaper term for top half of paper above horizontal fold

abscissa   co-ordinate running parallel to *x*-axis in 'coordinate graph' (qv)

abstract (as noun)   summary of book, periodical feature, report or learned paper

a/c   account mark, used on invoices, statements, etc; stands for 'account current'

accented (diacritical) signs   those commonly used in European languages are:

å	boll	ç	cedilla	č š ř	haček
è	grave	ô	circumflex	Ø	bar
é	acute	ñ	tilde	ä ö ü	umlaut

in addition, diaeresis (¨) is used in English to denote second of two adjacent vowels which is to be pronounced separately, as in 'naïve'

accordion fold   method of folding paper in which each fold is in opposite direction to previous one (see 'folding methods')

addendum (pl: addenda)   Latin for 'thing to be added'; used to denote item or items added subsequently to text of book

additive colour mixing   reproducing colours by mixing lights, as distinct from 'subtractive colour mixing' (qv):

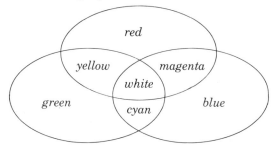

Adherography   trade name for duplicating process in which image is formed by adherence of powder (toner) to sticky, latent image

11

adjustable set-square/
triangle

drawing implement which pivots at one corner, calibrated to
provide desired angle of inclination:

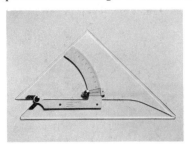

advance copies

limited quantity of new publication made up in advance of main
quantity for publicity, promotion or review purposes

agate line

unit of measurement used in US newspaper advertising to denote
column depth (14 agate lines = 1 inch)

AGI

initials of 'Alliance Graphique Internationale': world-wide clique of
well-known graphic designers and illustrators who gather together
from time to time for purpose of mutual admiration

AIGA

initials of 'American Institute of Graphic Arts', founded in 1914 in
New York to 'do all things which would raise the standard and the
extension and development towards perfection of the graphic arts in
the US'

airbrush

pressure gun with very fine nozzle, used for graded tone effects in
artwork, especially retouching of photographs

albumen plate

lithographic plate made from photographic negative using light-
sensitive coating, formerly containing white of egg (albumen); also
known as 'surface plate' as distinct from 'deep-etch plate' (qv)

ALGOL

see 'computer languages'

algorithmics

study of problem-solving by use of predetermined sets of procedural
instructions, as distinct from 'heuristics' (qv); 'algorithm' is one set
of fixed instructions for carrying out process, and may be either
'ordinary language algorithm' or 'computer algorithm'

alignment

lining up type or other graphic matter to common horizontal or
vertical line (but see also 'ranged') sometimes spelled 'alinement'

12

alignment chart	same as 'nomogram' (qv)
all-in-hand	state of typesetting job after all copy has been passed out to compositors
all-up	state of print job after all copy has been set
alphanumeric set	strictly speaking, set of alphabetic letters and numerals, but may also be stretched to include other signs, such as + =
ammonia duplication process	form of 'diazo' (qv) process in which latent image is made visible by exposure to evaporating ammonia
ampersand	symbol for 'and' derived from fusion of words in Latin word *et*:

selection of ampersands

anaglyph	composite stereoscopic picture printed in superimposed, complementary colours for viewing through special coloured spectacles
analog computer	one devised to represent variables in problems and to construct conceptual models (analogs) of them; note that alternate spelling 'analogue' is not now used in this context
angles	types of angles are:

acute angle: *right angle:* *obtuse angle:* *reflex angle:*
less than 90° *90°* *more than 90°* *more than 180°*

animation	representation of motion by sequential photography of series of images on cinefilm or videotape; may be computer-generated
animation stand	another name for 'rostrum' (qv); more common in US
answer print	in cinefilm, first projection print of new film, submitted to film maker by process lab before more copies are made; also known as 'approval print'
Antiqua	German term denoting 'roman type' as distinct from 'black letter'

antique paper	unsized, or lightly sized, material with rough, matt finish, usually bulky; used mainly for books
aperture (of camera lens)	opening of lens of camera, varied in diameter (unless fixed) by means of diaphragm (iris); size of aperture is indicated by '*f*-number', often called '*f* stop' and is one factor in calculating exposure time:

  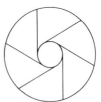

fully open at f2.8 *stopped down to f5.6* *stopped down to f11*

aperture card	one having inset frame or frames for filing and viewing 'microfilm' (qv)
appendix (pl: appendices)	part of 'end-matter' of book, usually for purpose of enlarging on some element in text or to give supporting statistics
approval print	in cinefilm, same as 'answer print' (qv)
arabic numerals	symbols 1 2 3 4 5 6 7 8 0 as distinct from roman numerals; more properly 'hindu-arabic numerals', since they originated in India around 500AD, were adopted by Arabs about 900AD and Spanish by 1000AD:

area composition	in photocomposition, operation of setting made-up pages in varying formats for advertisements, tables, pages of periodicals and the like, following arrangement of these by use of 'video layout system' (qv)
art	may be used as abbreviation for 'artwork' (qv), especially in US, where it does not imply completeness
art paper	one with clay coating which becomes hard and smooth when passed through rollers

14

artwork	any matter prepared for photomechanical reproduction; known in US as 'mechanical' (qv) if complete
arty-farty	client's term for graphic design which is imaginative and innovatory
ASA	abbreviation for 'American Standards Association'; when prefixed to a number shown on film stock, it denotes relative 'film speed' (qv) for calculating exposure
asap, ASAP	initials of 'as soon as possible'; rather pointless phrase often appended to orders for photography, processing, print, etc
ascender	that part of certain lower-case letters, such as b, d, f, h, appearing above the 'x-height' (qv)
ascender line	imaginary horizontal line connecting tops of ascender letters, often (but not necessarily) corresponding to 'cap line' (qv)
aspect ratio	in cinefilm and TV, ratio of frame height to frame width: in 35mm cinefilm it is 3.155 : 4.34; in 16mm cinefilm, 2.94 : 4.10; and in TV, 3 : 4
asterisk	type character used as first order of 'reference marks' (qv) for footnotes; also used on occasion for unprintable words like f***
astonisher	printer's slang for exclamation mark (more common in US)
ATypI	acronym for *Association Typographique Internationale*, founded in 1957 'to bring about a better understanding of typography, a higher level of typographic design, and to secure international protection for typefaces'
author's correction	any correction, deletion or addition to proof which is not result of printer's error; known as 'author's alteration' in US (see 'AA')
autolithography	process of drawing directly onto lithographic stone or plate without use of photography
autopositive	photographic material or process which provides positive image of original without intervening negative stage
AVA	initials of 'audio-visual aids': woolly portmanteau term covering slide and film strip projectors, overhead projectors, closed-circuit TV and tape recorders, whether sound-vision linked or not

15

axonometric
projections

'orthographic projections' (qv) in which object is inclined in relation to picture plane, as distinct from 'multiview projections'; there are three forms:

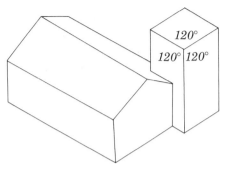

isometric projection: all three axes of rectilinear object drawn at equal angles; dimensions along them are to same scale

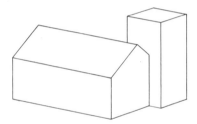

dimetric projection: dimensions to same scale on two of axes, different on third

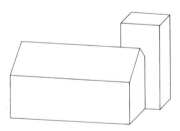

trimetric projection: dimensions to different scale along each axis

azure

term used for lighter tints of blue 'laid' and 'wove' papers (qv)

B

B (= bulb) — in photography, shutter setting on camera which holds shutter open as long as exposure release is held down

back (of book) — that edge of any book at which leaves are secured (see 'book'); also called 'spine' or 'shelfback'

back margin — see 'page'

back matter (of book) — US term for 'end-matter' (qv)

back projection — projecting transparencies onto back of translucent screen, fine cloth or frosted glass; used for faking backgrounds in studio photography:

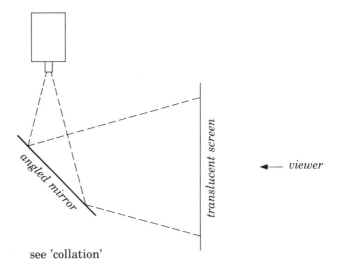

back-step collation — see 'collation'

back-up, backing-up — printing second, or reverse, side of sheet; also known as perfecting

backbone (of book) — same as 'spine' (qv)

backslanted — said of typeface which inclines to left:

ABCdefghijklmn

bang	slang for exclamation mark
bank paper	uncoated paper produced for typewriting, similar to bond but lighter; used for carbon copies
banker envelope	commonest pattern, having opening and flap on longer edge, thus:

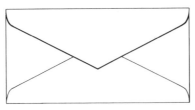

banner	newspaper headline running across whole width of page
bar code	pre-printed pattern of vertical lines which is 'read' by computer-linked optical sensor; such devices are now increasingly in use at checkout points of supermarkets for stock control and ordering, and pattern is devised to conform with Universal Product Code (UPC) which identifies country of origin, manufacturer and type of product
bar graph/chart	'coordinate graph' (qv) in which values are represented by vertical or horizontal bars, as distinct from line graph; also known as 'columnar graph': if more than one value is to be included, 'segmented bar graph' may be used:

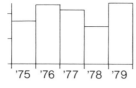 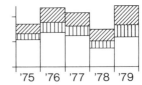

barn doors	in photography, apparatus fixed to spotlight or floodlamp to control direction of light:

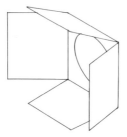

barrel printer	see 'computer output devices'
baryta paper	special matt-coated paper suitable for 'repro proofs' (qv)
base alignment (type)	in photocomposition, system in which different sizes of type set on same line are automatically aligned on base line: economic **on-line** information for the chemical industry.
base artwork	artwork to which further components (such as screened halftone positives) are to be added before reproduction
base film	in photomechanical reproduction, material to which film positives are stripped in order to make contact film for platemaking
baseline	horizontal line connecting the bottoms of those lower-case characters which do not have descenders, from which is derived 'baseline-to-baseline' method of measuring line intervals; see also 'x-height'
BASIC	see 'computer languages'
basis weight	US term for weight of 'ream' (qv) of paper to given standard size
bastard size	any matter used in printing which is of non-standard size
bastard title	same as 'half-title' (qv)
batter (as noun)	in letterpress, damaged type or block
Bauhaus	German for 'Building House': most famous design school of inter-war years, started in 1919 at Weimar, Germany, under Walter Gropius; moved to Dessau in 1925, Berlin in 1932, finally closed by Nazis in 1933
beard (of type)	in UK, space extending from base line of typeface to lower limit of body as it appears on page; in US, synonym for 'bevel' (see 'type')
bed (of press)	flat surface on which matter to be printed from is laid
begin even	instruction to printer: start copy full out, without indent
below-the-line	advertising term used to describe those items in an advertising budget which are not strictly advertisements, eg: brochures, promotion pieces

19

Benday tint	obsolete technique for applying mechanical tint to line plate
bevel (of type)	sloping surface which extends from shoulder to face (see 'type')
bevel (of letterpress plate)	another name for 'flange' (qv)
BFMP	see 'British Printing Industries Federation'
bf	instruction to printer on manuscript, typescript or proof: set in 'bold face' (more common in newspaper publishing)
biblio, biblio page	common name for page in book 'prelims' (qv) which contains publishing history of book and publisher's imprint; but beware of confusion with 'bibliography' (qv)
bibliography	list of authors, titles and publishers of books and periodicals relevant to particular subject; may form self-contained publication in its own right but is more normally part of 'end-matter' (qv) of another book
bimetal plate	long-lasting litho printing plate in which printing area is of copper and non-printing area of steel or aluminium; used for runs of 500,000 and over
binary code	system which can convert anything expressible as numbers or as symbolic logic into a sequence of 'yes/no' questions and answers for storage in, and retrieval from, a computer
binary digit	in computer usage, basic unit (either 1 or 0) of 'binary code' system (qv)
binary notation	two-state arithmetic employed in electronic computers because of 'on-off' modes typical of certain kinds of electronic circuit; digits used are 1 (on) and 0 (off) and values are represented by position of digits, thus:

```
0  0  0  0   position
8  4  2  1   value
```

decimal values may then be expressed in this way:

decimal	binary	decimal	binary	decimal	binary
0	0000	2	0010	4	0100
1	0001	3	0011	5	0101

6	0110	10	1010	14	1110
7	0111	11	1011	15	1111
8	1000	12	1100		
9	1001	13	1101		

binary coded decimal (BCD) system employs groups of four 'bits' each:

	thousands	hundreds	tens	units
8219 =	1000	0100	0001	1001
4601 =	0100	0110	0000	0001

binding edge   that edge of book at which sheets are secured; same as 'spine' and 'back edge'

binding methods   most common binding methods are:

loose-leaf methods

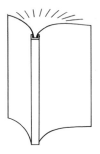 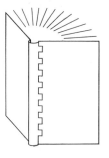 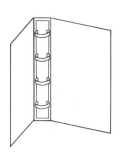 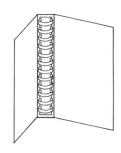

plastic grip spine   *plastic comb spine*   *post or ring binder*   *multiple ring binder*

permanent binding methods

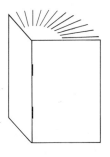 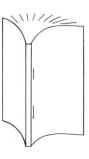 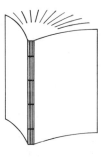 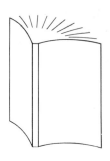

saddle-stitched   *side-stitched*   *section-sewn*   *perfect (unsewn)*

bit	useful contraction of '*binary digit*' (qv)
black crush	in TV, electronic effect which converts live action image into total black/white contrast, without half tones
black face	same as 'bold face' (qv)
black letter	style of typeface once widely used in northern Europe, closely based on broad-nib pen style; also known as 'gothic' (qv) in UK, 'Old English' and 'text type' in US:

𝔄𝔅𝔆𝔇𝔈𝔉𝔊𝔥𝔍𝔎
black and turquoise

blanket cylinder	in 'offset' (qv), one which takes ink image from 'plate cylinder' and transfers it to paper or other printing material by means of thick sheet of rubberized fabric
bleach-out	same as 'line conversion' (qv); also, under-developed photoprint with 'ghost' image, used as basis for line drawing
bleed	to run line or halftone image off edge of trimmed page or sheet; it is usual to allow 3mm for this
blind-embossed	relief impression made with die-stamp which is not inked or foiled
blind folio	page of book which does not have page number (folio) but which is included in pagination, eg: title page
blind P	reversed P with filled-in counter, used as 'paragraph mark' (qv)
Blissymbols	set of 100 signs devised by Charles Bliss, first published 1949 as basis of international non-phonetic language system but not given practical application until 1971
block	line or halftone plate mounted to 'type-height' (qv) for use in letterpress printing (term not common in US)
block book	one printed from page-sized wood blocks from which letters were carved in relief; fore-runner of movable type book

block diagram

1) one devised to represent functional relationships:

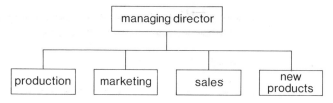

2) one using square blocks as units to represent comparisons of quantities:

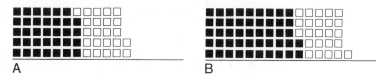

3) one used by cartographers to show geological and/or surface relief of particular portion of land:

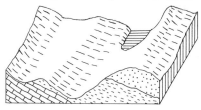

blocking

stamping image onto case of book or pack by means of blocking, or binder's, brass; may be inked, foiled or left blind (ie: without either); known in US as 'stamping' or 'tooling'

blockmaker

one who makes letterpress plates by 'photoengraving' (qv) known in US as 'photoengraver'

blow-moulding

forcing air between two sheets of plastic to form hollow shape; thus:

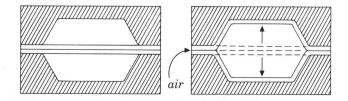

blues, blueprints	poor quality proofs, having white lines against blue ground, intended for preliminary checking purposes; largely superseded by 'diazo' prints (qv)
blurb	brief summary of contents of a book and/or potted biography of author printed on jacket or soft cover
body	main part of piece of 'type' (qv)
body copy/matter/type	text matter used in main body of work, as distinct from headings or other display matter
body size	measurement in points of body of type as cast; may be slightly larger than 'type size' (qv)
bold, bold face	heavier version of normal weight of typeface
bolt	any folded edge of printed section (signature) which is to be trimmed (ie: not back fold)
bond paper	grade of paper made for writing and typewriting, but which can also be used for printing; lighter weights are called 'bank'
book	any leaved work which is bound; parts of typical book are:

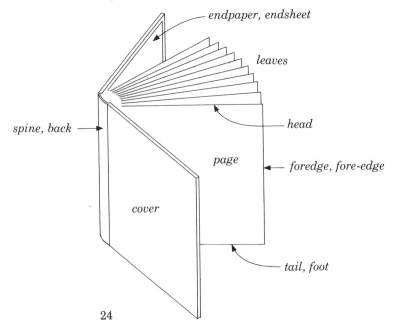

book jacket	printed paper outer, wrapped around cased cover of hard-backed book; also known as 'dust jacket' or 'wrapper'
book proof	'sheet proofs' (qv) made up in book form for final approval
book sizes	see 'paper sizes and subdivisions'
border (type)	ornamental type matter consisting of single pieces, cast to standard body sizes, arranged in strip form:

Boring's mother-in-law	famous ambiguous image devised by US psychologist E G Boring, which sometimes looks like old woman, sometimes like young girl:

bounce-lighting	in studio photography, lighting subject solely or mainly by indirect lighting reflected from walls, ceilings or specially made reflectors
bowl (of type)	curving stroke of type character enclosing counter (see 'type')
box	type or other graphic matter enclosed by rule border to separate it from other matter; also, that border itself

box enamel	'enamel paper' (qv) specially made for box covers
BP chromo	special grade of 'chromo' paper (qv) used for block-proofing
bpi	initials of 'bits per inch': measurement of density with which data can be recorded on magnetic tape (see 'bit')
brace	typographic sign used to link several items, thus:

$$\left.\begin{array}{l}\text{FARMDOC}\\\text{AGDOC}\\\text{PLASDOC}\end{array}\right\}\ \text{included in Central Patents Index (CPI) from 1970}$$

bracketed (type)	used to describe those serifs which are joined to main part (stem) of type character by continuous curve or bracket:

I

brackets	pair of signs like this (parentheses or curved brackets) or this [square brackets]; used to separate matter they enclose from context
BRAD	initials of 'British Rate & Data', regular publication giving those details of national and provincial newspapers published in UK which are relevant to placing of advertisements
brass	engraved plate used by bookbinder for 'blocking' (qv); known in US as 'binder's die'
break up for colour	instruction to printer: break up forme which is to be printed in more than one colour, making separate formes for each colour
breve	curved line over vowel indicating that it is 'short', thus: nĭppy
Brightype	trade name for technique of deriving photographic image from letterpress type or plates, by spraying on black lacquer, then removing it from face only, so providing reflective surface for photography
Bristol board	fine pasteboard with smooth surface, ideal for drawing up artwork

British Printing Industries Federation	employers' organization and trade association for general printing industry in UK, founded in 1900 as 'British Federation of Master Printers' (BFMP) and renamed in 1974; has displayed rather equivocal, unhelpful attitude to graphic design
broadside, broadsheet	any sheet in its basic, uncut size; one which is printed on one side only
bromide	short for 'bromide print': normal kind of photographic print; often used for pre-platemaking proofs in photolitho, hence 'bromide proofs'
brownprint	same as 'Van Dyke print' (qv)
BS	prefix used to denote standard set by British Standards Institution; there are shoals of these things in printing and publishing – far too many to list here (but see Bibliography)
buckram	sized bookbinders' cloth
bullet	type ornament in form of large dot, used to itemize or emphasize
butt splicing	in film and tape editing, making joins without overlaps by means of adhesive tape or heat fusion
by-line	typeline giving name of author(s) of periodical or newspaper article
byte	in computer jargon, group of 'bits' (qv) – usually 6 or 8 – which make up one alphabetic, numerical or special character

C

©	copyright mark, used to conform with 'Universal Copyright Convention 1952' (qv)
CAD	initials of 'computer aided design'
calenders	metal rollers through which paper is passed in order to give it smoothly polished (calendered) surface during making process
caliper	thickness of sheet, especially of board, measured in microns (millionths of a metre) or mils (thousandths of an inch)

calligraphy	fine handwriting
cameo (type)	applied to those typefaces in which characters are reversed white out of solid or shaded ground:

SPECIAL NEWS

camera-ready art(work)	any 'camera-ready copy' (qv) which includes hand work
camera-ready copy	any matter prepared for reproduction that is ready to go before 'process camera' (qv)
camera-ready paste-up	any camera-ready artwork which involves pasting together of number of component parts
camera shake	greatest enemy of sharp, crisp negative making: all shots not requiring hand holding should be made from tripod mounting to eliminate camera shake, especially at slower shutter speeds
camera types	main camera types are:

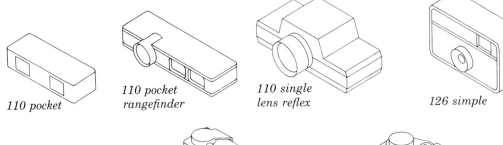

110 pocket   110 pocket rangefinder   110 single lens reflex   126 simple

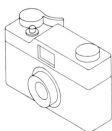

35mm compact

35mm compact rangefinder

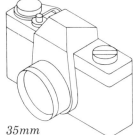

35mm single lens reflex

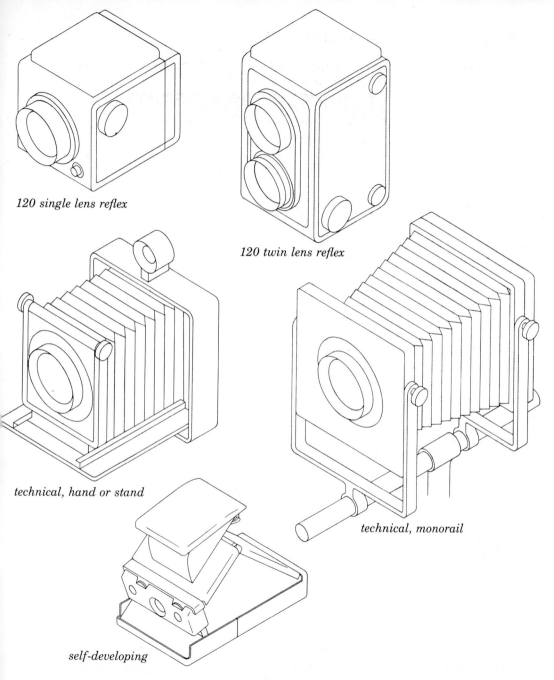

120 single lens reflex

120 twin lens reflex

technical, hand or stand

technical, monorail

self-developing

29

cancel (as noun)	reprinted leaf or section to be substituted for existing part of book which was printed in error
cancelled numeral (figure)	type character consisting of numeral with diagonal stroke through it; used in mathematical texts
capital, cap	upper-case letter, as A, B, C, D; also known as 'majuscule'
cap line	imaginary horizontal line connecting tops of line of caps, often (but not necessarily) corresponding to 'ascender line' (qv)
caption	descriptive phrase, sentence or paragraph placed below, beside or above illustration
carbon arc lamp	light source used in photomechanical reproduction and cine-projection, now largely replaced by 'metal halide lamp' (qv)
carbonless copy paper	same as 'ncr' paper (qv)
cardinal numbers	one, two, three and so on, as distinct from ordinal numbers, first, second, third
caret, caret mark	sign used in proof correction to show that something is to be inserted:

carᴧful   eᴧ

carry forward	same as 'take over' (qv)
Cartesian graph	same as 'coordinate graph' (qv)
cartogram	map which incorporates statistical information
carton	container designed to lie flat until required for use, as distinct from rigid box
cartridge (paper)	closely woven, well sized paper produced in heavy substances for drawing and offset litho printing; best grades are made on 'twin-wire' machines (qv)
case	stiff cover of book; also, container for type
case fraction	one cast as whole type, as distinct from 'piece fraction' or 'full-sized fraction' (qqv); also known as 'solid fraction'

cased/case-bound book	one with stiff cover as distinct from one with soft cover; same as 'hard back' or 'hard cover' book
casting-off	estimating amount of space manuscript will occupy when typeset in certain typeface and measure
cast coated	coated paper or board with exceptionally thick, glossy coating, achieved by adding second coating to pre-coated base and passing it round highly polished, heated drum to get high finish
catchline	identifying number and title set at top of each 'galley proof' (qv)
cathode ray tube	see 'CRT'
CCTV	initials of 'closed circuit television' (qv)
CdS meter	see 'exposure meter'
cedilla c	see 'accented (diacritical) signs'
Ceefax (= see facts)	name of British Broadcasting Corporation's system for transmitting 'teletext' (qv) news and information
cel	in film animation, transparent surface of same proportion as frame of cinefilm, on which one stage of animation sequence is drawn; of standard size and punched to fit over register pins:

cel sandwich	in film animation, superimposition of up to four cels for simultaneous photography
cell	in 'photogravure' (qv), tiny recessed dot carrying inked image, similar to halftone dot

31

cellophane	proprietary name for brand of cellulose film; transparent, grease-proof material used mainly for wrapping
centered dot	US expression for raised point used for decimal notation
centre fold/spread	central opening of section across two pages
cf	abbreviation for *confer*, Latin for 'compare'; used in footnotes
chad	paper waste produced when holes are punched in paper tape or cards
chain lines/marks	widely spaced watermark lines in 'laid' paper (qv) running at right angles to closely spaced 'laid' lines
chain printer	see 'computer output devices'
chancery italic	roman handwriting style of 15–16th century, on which cursive (italic) typefaces were based:

*Dele uarie forti de littere poi, che in questo Tratta-
tello trouerai, se io ti uolessi ad una per una descriuere*

chapel	old term for association of journeyman printers, now applied to local branches of printers' and journalists' trades unions
chapter drop	position on page of book at which text begins below chapter head, as distinct from standard run of text
character	any individual letter, figure, punctuation mark or sign in typeface
character assembly	blanket term covering all methods by which letters, figures, special characters and spaces are generated for reproduction; more suitable than 'typesetting' for such techniques as photocomposition
character count	sum of characters in line or paragraph or piece of copy
character generator	central part of computer-aided CRT photocomposition system; two basic types are (a) character projection and (b) character formation
character set	set of letters, numerals (figures), punctuation marks, reference marks and other signs, chosen or designed for particular system or keyboard; in typesetting, character set is known as 'fount' (qv)

32

chase	in letterpress, metal frame used to hold and secure matter for printing; hence 'in chase' (ready to print)
chemical pulp	wood pulp chemically treated, as distinct from mechanical pulp; used for better quality printing papers
chemical transfer process	same as 'DTR' (qv)
chroma	degree of intensity or purity of any colour; also, in TV, abbreviation for 'chrominance': colour component of video signal
chromo	one-sided art paper used mainly for proofing
chromolithography	traditional technique of drawing images on stone (autolithography) in matched sets to produce multi-coloured picture; hand-drawn colour lithography persisted to mid-twentieth century, especially for posters
Cibachrome-A	speedy colour print system working directly positive-to-positive
cicero	'Didot' (qv) equivalent of 'pica' as unit of measurement: 4.500mm (see also 'corps douze')
circular graph	one in which values are plotted from central point along radiating axes, forming closed curves:

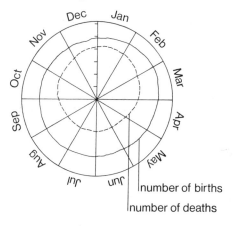

circumflex — see 'accented (diacritical) signs'

clarendon	family of typefaces having characteristics both of roman and slab-serif:

ABDegh

clean proof	one containing no errors or corrections
clicker	slang for compositor who has responsibility of passing out copy for setting by fellow comps
client	person who wants everything yesterday and at half-price
client's rough	common misnomer for 'presentation visual' (qv)
closed circuit television	system in which signal is fed to limited number of viewing monitors by cable
closed 'h'	lower-case italic 'h' in which short stroke curves inwards, thus:

b

closed section/signature	one in which folds or bolts are left uncut
clump	in letterpress, spacing material of 6pt body or thicker (also called 'slug' in US); wooden clumps are known as 'reglets'
CMC7	character set designed for 'MICR' (qv)
coarse screen	any halftone screen up to 85 lines to inch (34 lines to centimetre)
coated (art) paper	one having covering of coating slip made from china clay; may be 'machine', 'blade' or 'cast' coated
COBOL	see 'computer languages'
cock-and-hens	brace composed of several pieces of type joined together; central piece is cock, end pieces are hens
cock-up numeral (figure) or letter	same as 'superior numeral (figure) or letter' (qv)

34

cocked-up initial	one projecting above line of type on which it stands, thus:

Punched card data processing is based upon the unit record pr
one card is utilized for encoding the essential data of each trans.
data are recorded and verified through some type of data recor
automatic punching, as indicated in the previous chapter. The ne

cold composition	imprecise and regrettable term intended to cover any composition produced by typewriters but extended to include photocomposition
cold type	another loose term meaning same as 'cold composition'
collation	to check correct order of printed sections (signatures) after gathering; also used (incorrectly) to include whole process of gathering and collation, especially of single sheets; collating marks are often printed in stepped sequence on back folds of sections (known as 'back-steps') so that any misplacement is easily spotted:

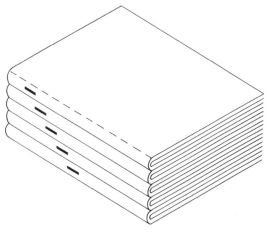

collotype	photomechanical, planographic printing process using gelatin covered plate without halftone dot; very fine reproduction but only suited to short runs
colophon	device used as distinguishing mark by publisher, usually printed on title page and blocked on spine of book
colour (of typeface)	degree of lightness or heaviness in appearance of particular typeface

colour bars	in four-colour processing, proofs should contain standard sets of bars devised to show strength of ink across plate, register, etc
colour-coding	distinguishing between groups of products, printed forms, signs or what-have-you by giving them different colours; popular technique of doubtful effectiveness (what about differing light conditions and people with varying degrees of colour blindness?)
colour negative film	film in which colours are in negative form after processing
colour positives	set of screened four-colour separations with positive image, used for deep-etch litho platemaking
colour reversal film	film in which colours are in positive (natural) form after processing
colour separation	photographic filtering process whereby colours of an original are separated out for reproduction
colour separations	see 'separation artwork'
colour stat	rough colour print suitable for use in presentation
colour temperature	expression in degrees Kelvin (°K) of colour quality of light source, derived from appearance of light radiated by black body heated to incandescence
colour transparency	colour photograph (usually positive) on transparent film
columnar graph	see 'bar graph/chart'
combination fraction	addition of superior and inferior numerals to 'diagonal fraction' (qv) to provide greater variety, thus:
combination plate	see 'line-and-halftone plate'
command	operating instruction to computer
commercial A	type character meaning 'at': @
communication theory	mathematical theory relating to least number of decisions required to identify one message from given set of messages
comp	common abbreviation for 'comprehensive': US term for 'presentation visual' (qv)

compact-source iodide lamp	see 'metal halide lamp'
compose	to put together type and rules by hand or machine
composing room	that part of printing works where type is set and made up
composing stick	implement for setting type in by hand
composite print	in cinefilm, same as 'married print' (qv)
composition size	any size of type up to 14pt used primarily for text setting
compositor, comp	one who composes and imposes type; also called 'typographer' in US
compound table	in film animation, US term for 'rostrum table' (qv)
computer console	unit used for all manual communication with computer; contains display of information and has keyboard for input of instructions
computer graphics	any computer-generated output which is not alphanumeric may be defined as graphic but term is particularly applied to graphic forms uniquely or most effectively produced by this means:

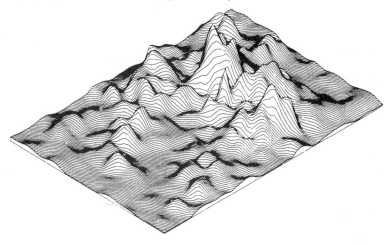

computer input devices	those by which human instructions or queries are made intelligible to computer, available in following types: punched card, paper tape, teletypewriter, optical character recognition (OCR) encoder,

magnetic ink character recognition (MICR) encoder, visual display unit (VDU) with light-pen, digitizing pad (tablet) or table

computer output devices
: those by which information from computer is made intelligible to humans, available in following types: teletypewriter, high-speed impact line-printers (barrel or chain), non-impact printers (ink-jet, electrothermal, electrostatic, dot-matrix or xerographic), graph plotters (flatbed or drum), visual display unit (VDU), microfilm

computer languages
: several languages have been developed specially for use in computer programming, among which are: ALGOL (ALGOrithmic Language); COBOL (COmmon Business Oriented Language); FORTRAN (FORmula TRANslator); PL/1 (Programming Language/One); BASIC (Beginners' All-purpose Symbolic Instruction Code)

computerized composition
: character assembly with aid of computer which is programmed to process some, or all, functions after keyboarding and up to setting

concertina fold
: method of folding paper in which each fold is in opposite direction to previous one (see 'folding methods'); same as 'accordion fold'

condensed
: used to describe narrower version of normal typeface

cone of clear vision
: central cone of normal human vision in which we see clearly, taken to be angle of 2 degrees

cone of vision (perspective)
: in 'perspective projections' (qv), configuration formed by convergence of 'visual rays' onto 'station point'

conic sections
: curves derived from planes intersecting a cone; they are:

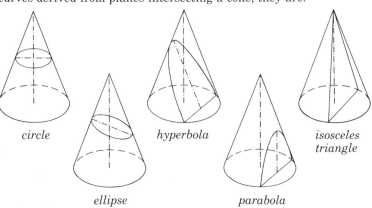

circle

ellipse

hyperbola

parabola

isosceles triangle

conical projections (global)   group of projections of Earth in which plane of projection is cone which touches globe along parallel:

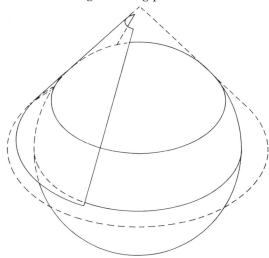

contact print   photographic print made direct from film positive or negative without enlargement

contact printing frame   same as 'vacuum frame' (qv)

contact screen   another name for 'halftone screen' (qv)

continuous fold   system of folding paper from roll in series of concertina folds (see 'folding methods')

continuous-tone copy   any original in which the gradation of tones requires photomechanical halftone processing

contre-jour   in photography, shooting with light source in front of camera lens rather than to one side or to rear:

control loop

in 'ergonomics' (qv), symbolic relationship between operator and machine he/she controls:

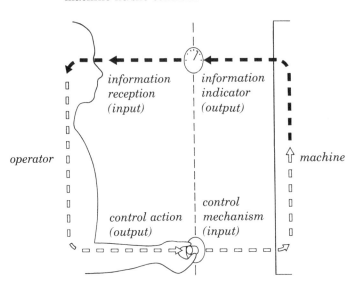

operator

information reception (input)

information indicator (output)

machine

control action (output)

control mechanism (input)

converging verticals

familiar visual phenomenon in which parallel vertical lines appear to converge (as when tall building is viewed from below); corrected by use of 'rising front' (qv) on camera:

converting

making envelopes, pads, paper bags, cardboard tubes and similar articles in which there is little or no printing as such

coordinate graph

representation of relation between two (sometimes three) variable quantities by plotting series of points (usually joined) along axes known as coordinates:

40

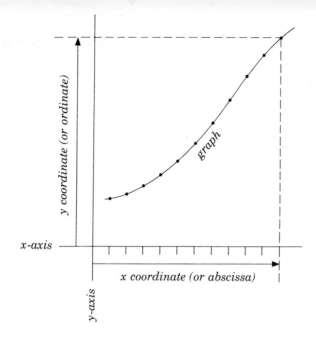

cool colours	green or blue, or colours which are predominantly green or blue
copperplate printing	short-run 'intaglio' (qv) process whereby polished plate is lightly etched so as to carry ink, characterised by sharpness of image, intensity of blacks and slight raised effect; used for visiting and invitation cards
copy	either typewritten matter for typesetting, or all matter intended for reproduction, depending on context
copyfitting	same as 'casting-off' (qv)
copyholder	proof reader who reads aloud from original copy whilst another checks proof
copyreader	US term for one who sub-edits copy (known in UK as 'sub-editor'
copyright	see 'Universal Copyright Convention 1952'
copytaster	one who selects items for possible inclusion in newspaper
corner marks	'trim marks' (qv) on artwork, indicating corners for trimming

corporate identity	same as 'house style' (qv) but sounds posher
corps douze	French equivalent of '12pt' as body size of type (see also 'cicero')
corrigendum (pl: corrigenda)	Latin for 'thing to be corrected'; used to describe item or items corrected subsequent to printing of main part of book
counter	space enclosed by closed parts of type characters such as a b d e g o
counting keyboard	in photocomposition, input device which keeps tally of operator's position in line, thus requiring him/her to make 'end-of-line' decisions (qv), as distinct from 'non-counting' keyboard
cover	any paper, board or other material made up to form outside of book
CPA	initials of 'critical path analysis', method of approaching task by using arrow diagram which sets out planning, analysis, scheduling and control functions in clear sequences:

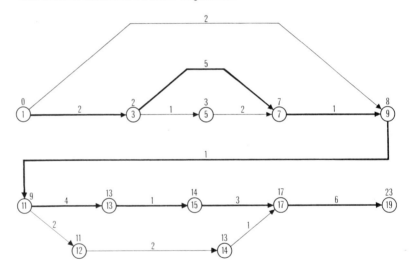

cpi	initials of 'characters per inch'; measure of information which can be accommodated on magnetic tape, drum or disc
CPM	initials of 'critical path method'; same as 'CPA' (qv)
cps	initials of 'characters per second'; rate at which machine such as 'teleprinter' (qv) will operate (range is from 12–120cps)

CPU	initials of 'central processor unit'; that part of computer comprising main memory, control unit and arithmetic unit
crease	to impress paper or board so that it may be more easily folded; same as 'scoring'
crop, cropmark	lines drawn on overlay to show printer which part of photograph is to be used for printed image; see also 'scaling'
cross front	in photography, facility in camera which allows lens to be moved laterally in relation to film, in similar fashion to 'risng front' (qv)
cross symbols	some types of cross symbols are:

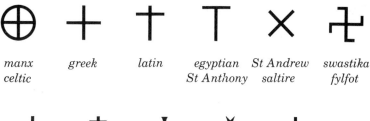

manx   *greek*   *latin*   *egyptian*   *St Andrew*   *swastika*
celtic   *St Anthony*   *saltire*   *fylfot*

patriarchal   *papal*   *St George*   *maltese*   *Lorraine*

crosshead	sub-heading located between paragraphs of text matter in periodical or newspaper; equivalent to 'sub-heading' in book parlance
cross-line screen	same as 'halftone screen' (qv)
cross-stemmed 'W'	one like this:

W

crown	see 'paper sizes'

CRT abbreviation for 'cathode ray tube'; standard display device in electronic information-handling system, producing visible image on phosphor screen by directed beam of electrons:

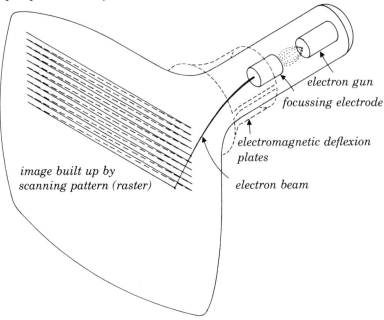

electron gun

focussing electrode

electromagnetic deflexion plates

image built up by scanning pattern (raster)

electron beam

cuneiform wedge-shaped, hence applied to writing of ancient inscriptions on clay tablets

cursive used of typeface resembling handwriting, particularly one developed from 'chancery italic' (qv); see also 'script'

cursor (of VDU) moving spot, cross or other symbol showing operator next input point on display

cut contraction of 'woodcut', later applied to any illustration from relief printing plate or block; now common in US as synonym for 'block'

cut flush book cover which is trimmed flush with leaves

cutaway shot in cinefilm and TV, one away from main action, often used to cover for omitted part of action (see also 'reaction shot')

cutline US term for caption under an illustration (cut = letterpress block) cut-out (halftone)   another name for 'silhouette halftone' (qv)

cut-out animation   in film animation, technique in which flat, cut-out shapes, sometimes with articulated joints, are moved manually between single stop-frame exposures

cutting copy   in cinefilm, print used for editing, usually from 'rushes', and from which is produced first 'rough-cut', then 'fine-cut' copy; called 'workprint' in US

cyan   blue/green colour containing no red; one of three primaries used in 'subtractive colour mixing' (qv)

cybernetics   study of control, communication and self-correction in mechanisms

cylinder press   printing machine using impression cylinder, as distinct from 'platen press':

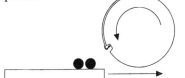

cylindrical projections   group of projections of Earth in which plane of projection is cylinder assumed to touch globe along one parallel (usually equator):

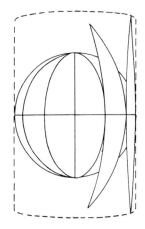
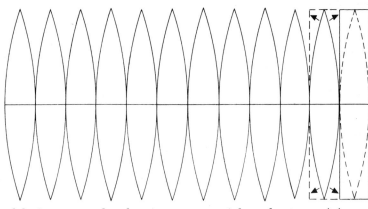

globe is segmented and segments are straightened out, remaining joined only at equator; segments are then converted into rectangles so that they adjoin along their whole length

continued overleaf

cylindrical projections
(continued)

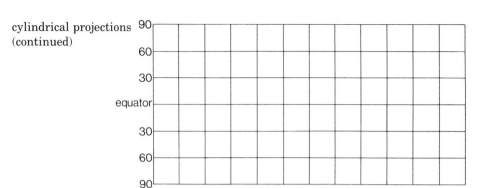

plate carrée: areas exaggerated and distorted towards poles

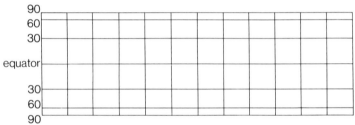

equal area orthographic: areas equal but badly distorted towards poles

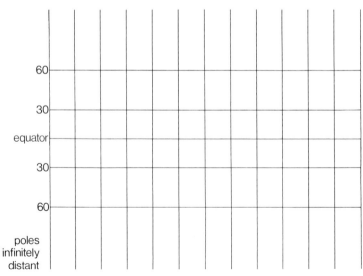

Mercator's: suitable only for navigation; hopelessly distorted land masses

Cyrillic alphabet	used throughout USSR; descended from Greek, devised in 9th century to incorporate characters expressing sounds peculiar to Slav tongue; not used for printing types until 18th century

D

dagger	type character used as second order of reference marks (qv) in footnotes; sometimes called 'obelisk' or 'long cross'
daisy wheel printer	typewriter employing flat, circular typing element known as 'daisy wheel' much used in 'word processor' systems (qv)
dandy roll	cylinder of wire gauze on papermaking machine which imparts pattern of wiremarks onto paper
data	factual information; used in data processing, especially of information held in memory store of computer; though properly plural (singular: datum) many authorities now treat 'data' as singular collective noun
data bank	information store in computer
database	in computer usage, large store of information organized so that all users draw on one common body of knowledge, eg: World Patent Index, typically accessed by combinations of 'keywords' (qv)
data carrier	in data processing, any medium, such as magnetic tape or paper tape, used for recording data
data processing	handling of information in mechanical, electromechanical and electronic systems
data matrix	array of quantities set out in columns and rows, representing variable and values they may take
date line	line of type at head of newspaper item, giving day, date and place of origin of news item if not local
datum	known or given fact (singular of 'data')
daylight film	colour film for use in daylight, fluorescent light or flashlight

De Stijl	Dutch for 'The Style'; art and design movement originating in Netherlands in 1917, advocating principles (eg: asymmetry, use of primary colours, emphasis on rectilinear forms) which have had immense influence on development of graphic design
dead matter (type)	set matter no longer intended for use, as distinct from 'live matter'
dead metal	non-printing areas in letterpress engraving
decal	printed transfer with adhesive back, now usually made in plastics
deckle edge	ragged edge of handmade paper, sometimes simulated on machine-made paper
deep-etched halftone	letterpress plate of screened halftone subject, in which additional etching is carried out to eliminate halftone dot completely in selected areas
deep-etch plate	lithographic plate made from photographic positive as distinct from albumen plate (qv); image is slightly recessed below surface of plate, allowing thicker film of ink to be carried in recesses and permitting longer print runs
delete	proof instruction to remove letter, word, phrase, sentence or paragraph crossed through, indicated by symbol:

too∅ much　　　　　Ꮟ

depth of field	in photography, zone of acceptable sharpness in front of and behind a subject on which camera is focussed; depth of field is affected by relative distance of object from camera, focal length (qv) of lens, and aperture (qv) of lens:

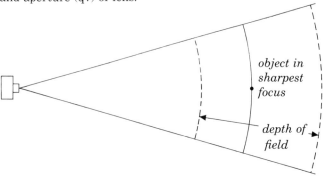

object in sharpest focus

depth of field

depth of field at f2.8   *stopped down to f11*

depth of focus	in photography, range of positions of film in relation to lens, in which acceptably sharp focus can be obtained:

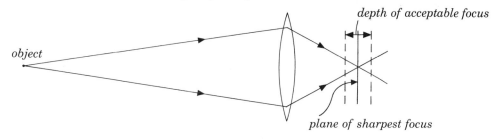

descender	that part of certain lower-case letters, such as g p q y appearing below 'x-height' (qv)
descender line	imaginary horizontal line connecting bottoms of descender letters
design assistant	1) one who does work for which senior designer takes credit 2) one who claims to know more about design in six weeks than senior designer has learned in sixteen years
Design Council	State sponsored body founded 1944 as Council of Industrial Design to promote cause of 'good' (?) design in British Industry but sadly crippled by dependence on financial support from industry
detail paper	thin, hard, semi-transparent paper used for sketches and layouts
Dewey Decimal Classification	devised by Melvil Dewey in 1876 to classify areas of knowledge, divided into ten main, numbered classes (eg: philosophy = 100) and sub-divided progressively into ten sub-classes, each of which is divided into ten sub-sub-classes, and so on; still in use (in modified form) in libraries all over the world (see also 'UDC')

diacritical mark/sign	one used to differentiate sounds or values of character; see 'accented (diacritical) signs'
diaeresis	see 'accented (diacritical) signs'
diagonal fraction	one like this: $^1/_3$, as distinct from one like this: $\frac{1}{3}$
diagonal scale	method by which existing scale may be used to derive another by extending parallels, thus:

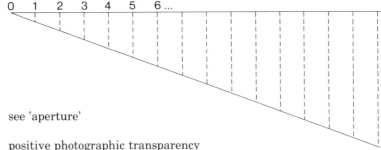

diaphragm (of camera)	see 'aperture'
diapositive	positive photographic transparency
diascope	projector of transparent subject matter such as diapositives or slides; also called 'slide projector' (but see also 'overhead projector')
diazo	limited-quantity reproduction process in which transparent or translucent original exposed to light source produces image on light-sensitive material (paper, cloth or film), which is developed by liquid, ammonia vapour or heat; prints can be black, blue or other colours (abbreviation of 'diazonium')
Didot point	typographic measurement system established in 1775 by French typefounder François Didot, now used in most European countries as alternative to Anglo-American point system; Didot point is now accepted as 0.375mm (0.0148in)
die-cutting	cutting paper or board by means of steel blades made up on forme; used in packaging and display work
die-stamping	stamping out raised, usually coloured, impression on paper or board by means of matched dies
digital computer	one which operates on information presented to it in binary digits, to make calculations of the kind required in, for example, photocomposition

50

digitize to render image into coded signal which can be processed electronically and used to reconstruct image in digitized form; images may be prepared in advance for electronic processing, or modified during scanning:

non-digitized numerals superimposed on grid

gridded numerals as recognized by scanner

digital numerals as stored for retrieval

digitizing pad input device on-line to digital computer, on which free-handing drawing is translated almost immediately into digitized form visible

visible on linked CRT; also known as 'tablet':

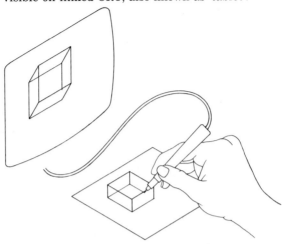

digram, digraph | group of two letters which represent one sound, as in 'ph' of digra*ph*

dimensioning | to avoid confusion, terms used in dimensioning representations of three-dimensional objects are: 'length', 'width', 'height'; 'depth' is not recommended

dimetric projection | see 'axonometric projections'

DIN | initials of *Deutsche Industrie Norm:* standard published by the German standards institution, which gave birth to the DIN (now ISO) paper size standards and to the DIN film speed ratings

dingbat | type ornament such as star, flash, fist or bullet (US term)

dinky-dash | same as 'jim-dash' (qv); more common in US

diphthong | union of two vowels pronounced in one syllable, as in 'loud', 'coil'; commonly used to describe 'ligature' (qv) of two vowels, as in 'æ', 'œ', though these should more properly be called 'monophthongs'

direct-entry photocomposition | system combining input, output and computer, in which type is set as copy is keyed in

direct image master | short-run litho plate, usually made from paper (hence 'paper plate') or plastic which is typed on directly

direct impression	form of type composition using typewriter; also known as 'typewriter composition', 'strike-on composition' and 'cold composition'
dirty proof	one containing many errors or corrections
disc (matrix)	in photocomposition, an image-carrier in disc form
display matter	any type matter not part of body of the text
display size	any size of type above 14pt, as distinct from 'text size' or 'composition size'
dissolve	in cinefilm and TV, 'fade-in' superimposed on 'fade-out' (qv)
distribute, dis, diss	to break up composed type and melt it down or return it to case
ditto marks	signs used to indicate repeat of what is on line above, thus: .. .. ..
dittogram/dittograph	repeated letter within word, caused by typesetting error
divided circle	see 'pie graph'
DL	envelope size in ISO Series of 110 × 220mm; will conveniently accommodate A4 sheet folded twice on long edge to 99 × 210mm
doctor blade	in photogravure, flexible metal blade which scrapes excess ink from surface of plate or cylinder before printing, leaving ink only in 'cells'
documentary	term coined in late 'twenties by Scottish film maker John Grierson to describe work of American film maker Robert Flaherty, which focussed on real people engaged in real-life tasks and pursuits, and containing a large measure of social concern; later extended to include similar work in still photography
dodging	in photography, controlling exposure in printing by partial masking of selected portion of print under enlarger
dog's cock	printer's slang for exclamation mark
dolly shot	in cinefilm and TV, one made with camera mounted on special wheeled truck
dope sheet	in cinefilm and TV graphics, chart listing order of cels, etc, against

	sequence of shots, instructions for panning, tracking, zooming, mixing or fading, and time required for these; more commonly known in US as 'exposure sheet'
dot-for-dot reproduction	making line facsimile from existing screened image of continuous tone subject, for further reproduction without re-screening
dot matrix	generally, any array from which pattern of dots may be selected to form image, specifically, one used as basis for character formation in 'matrix printer' (qv)
double dagger	type character used as third order of 'reference marks' (qv); also known as 'diesis' or 'double obelisk'
double-dot halftone	'duotone' (qv), especially one in which both impressions are in same colour
double-headed	in cinefilm, running separate picture and sound track simultaneously on editing machine or projector, to judge effect before transcribing sound onto 'optical track' (qv)
downstroke (of type)	heavy stroke in type character, derived from downward movement of pen in calligraphy:

drawing-on cover	attaching cover to paperback or periodical by glueing to spine and to part of end leaves (see also 'wrappering cover')
driving out	spacing words to fill line of type; widely practised in times past by printers because they were paid by number of lines set
drop cap	in typesetting, initial at beginning of text which is set in larger size of type, extending into lines of type below:

However carefully the arrangement of solidly s
matter may have been planned, with reference t
size and measure, for example, and however ca
that matter is subsequently set, it can almost always be
even more readable by sensible leading.

drop-down	same as 'chapter drop' (qv)
drop(ped)-out halftone	one in which halftone dot has been eliminated from highlight areas to give more brilliant result; also known as 'highlight halftone'
drop-tone, drop-out	same as 'line conversion' (qv)
dropped initial	same as 'drop-cap' (qv)
drum (matrix)	in photocomposition, an 'image-carrier' (qv) in drum form
drum plotter	computer output device in which writing tool moves laterally across width of roll of paper which is at same time being rotated on drum, thus permitting reasonably accurate reproduction of drawings, though not as good as 'flat-bed plotter' (qv)
dry offset	same as 'letterset' (qv)
dry transfer	see 'transfer lettering'
DTR	initials of 'diffusion-transfer-reversal': reprographic process which produces both negative and positive copy in single processing step; also known as 'chemical transfer'
duck-foot quotes	another name for 'guillemets' (qv)
dummy	sample made up to show format, substance and bulk of intended publication; may also include some graphic representation of print matter, thus forming 'presentation visual' (qv)
duotone	matched set of two halftones, each of same subject but with different 'screen angles' (qv); varying effects can be got by making one halftone more contrasty than its mate (sometimes called 'duograph')
dupe	slang for duplicate
duplex board	one consisting of two layers of different colour and/or quality, pasted together
duplex halftone	same as duotone, now less used
duplex mould	one used to hold two character matrices on typecasting machines
duplicator paper	soft, absorbent material for use with duplicating machine

dust wrapper/jacket	same as 'book jacket' (qv)
dye-based ink	one in which colour is derived from aniline dye
dye transfer print	photographic colour print of high quality made from either opaque or transparent colour original; very suitable for retouching for photomechanical reproduction and for one-off display prints
dyeline	same as 'diazo' (qv)

E13B	character set – consisting only of numerals and some signs – specially designed for 'MICR' (qv)
ear (of type)	small projection at top right of lower-case g
ear (of newspaper)	small display element on either side of newspaper 'nameplate' (qv)
easel binder	one which is constructed to be arranged for display of contents:

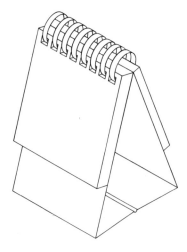

edge-notched card index	hand-sorting, coordinate indexing system in which holes along one or more edges of file card are given coded meaning; some holes are converted into notches by clipping away that part of card between

card edge and hole, so that, when needle or rod is inserted into pack of cards and raised, notched cards are left below:

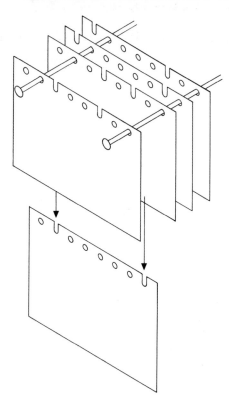

editing machine

in cinefilm, one on which film can be run at projection speed, together with one or more separate sound tracks; also allows editor to stop or reverse run and allows easy access to film for cutting

editing terminal

device using cathode ray tube (CRT) to display and correct key-boarded input in tape-stored photocomposition before printing out

edition

complete output of publication from one set of printing formes, whether in one impression or several; 'new edition' implies some change in content and/or style of production

edition-bound

same as 'cased' or 'case-bound' (qv); US term not so common in UK

eg

initials of *exempli gratia*, Latin for 'for example'

egyptian	name at first applied to both sans-serif and slab-serif typefaces by early nineteenth century founders, later reserved for slab-serifs; also known as 'antique'
eight-sheet	poster size 60 × 80in (153 × 203cm)
EL	initials of 'eye level' (see 'perspective projections')
electromagnetic spectrum	complete series of those wave forms which travel through space at speed of light; visible spectrum is one portion of this
electrostatic processes	those involving phenonemon of static electricity (see 'xerography')
electrotype, electro	duplicate letterpress plate made from an original plate by electro-plating process
elite (typewriter)	smaller of two commonest 'typewriter faces' (qv)
ellipse	in practical terms, any oblique view of circle, but see 'conic sections', also 'super ellipse'
ellipsis	sign used to indicate that something has been left out of phrase or sentence, thus . . .
em	in typesetting, dimension derived from square of any given type size, so that 8pt em is 8pts × 8pts, and so on; width of type lines, type areas, etc are given in 'pica ems' (qv)
em-quad	type space which is square of type size; colloquially known as 'mutton'
em-rule	one used to indicate omission of word, or—by some—to open and close parenthetical phrase, as alternative to spaced 'en-rule' (qv)
embossing	producing raised impression on board or paper, usually by 'die-stamping' (qv)
emulsion	essential light-sensitive coating on photographic materials; 'emulsion-side' of film is the dull one
en	half the width of an em (qv); as average width of a type character, it is useful unit for costing and copyfitting calculation
en-quad	type space half width of 'em-quad' (qv); colloquially known as 'nut'

en-rule	one used to denote 'and' as in 'man–machine interface', 'to' as in 'Paris–London flight' or – when spaced – to open and close parenthetical phrase
enamel paper	one-sided, highly finished coated paper used for box covers and colour proofing
end-of-line decisions	in type composition, those decisions which must be made at end of line of text in regard to justification and word-breaks; traditionally such decisions are made by compositor but it is now possible to program computer to make many of them
end even	instruction to compositor: end 'take' on full line
end-matter (of book)	those contents of book which follow main body of text, more correctly (but less commonly) called 'subsidiaries', also (in US) 'back matter' and 'postlims'; following sequence is offered as reasonable but not immutable:

appendices   acknowledgements (or could be in prelims)
author's notes   index
glossary   imprint (more usually in prelims)
bibliography

endoscope	see 'fibre optics'
endpapers	sheets at each end of cased book which are used to fasten leaves to cover; also known as 'endleaves' or (in US) 'endsheets'
epidiascope	projector for either transparent or opaque subject matter
episcope	projector for opaque subject matter such as pages of books
ergonomics	study of people in their working environments in relation to design of machine controls, work spaces and methods, information devices and all such factors affecting efficiency, comfort and health
erratum (pl: errata)	item omitted from publication, acknowledged by subsequent inclusion of erratum/errata slip
eszett	German language character representing 'ss': β
etching	harnessing of chemical effect of acid on metal to produce printable image

etaoin shrdlu	in typesetting, letters on first two vertical rows of keys on Linotype and other linecasting machines; used by typesetter to indicate that line will be reset or discarded
et seq	abbreviation for *et sequens,* Latin for 'and the following'
Euler circle	see 'Venn diagram'
even working	piece of print which is contained in sections of 16, 32, 48 or 64 pages, with no need for odd 4 or 8 page section
exception dictionary	in computer-aided photocomposition, memory store of word-breaks which do not conform to standard pattern
exotic (typeface)	traditionally applied by European printers to any typeface which does not conform to Latin letter forms, eg: Arabic
expanded/extended	used to describe wider version of normal typeface
exposure meter	in photography, device for making light readings to aid calculation of exposure time, employing one of three types of photocell: selenium, cadmium sulphide (CdS) or silicon blue
exposure sheet	in film animation, US term for 'dope sheet' (qv)
extremes	in film animation, drawings made at significant points in movements of animated subjects; also known as 'keys':

extreme   *in-betweens*

in-betweens   *extreme*

eye-legible copy	used of microform record which contains title or other lettering legible to naked eye

F

f-number, f stop	see 'aperture'
face	printing surface of type; also, design of type, hence 'typeface'
facetted classification	system of identifying elements in collection of information – such as book – so that they can be compared with elements defined by person seeking information, as distinct from less flexible systems such as 'Dewey' (qv) or UDC; very suited to punched-card or edge-notched card sorting
facsimile, facsim	exact copy, especially of manuscript, print matter or work of art, with no reduction or enlargement
fade-in, fade-out	in cinefilm and TV, changing from black to picture (fade-in) or picture to black (fade-out)
family (typeface)	complete range of design variants of particular typeface
fan-fold	mechanical folding method for continuous stationery
fast emulsion	in photography, one needing less exposure
fat face	roman typeface in which contrast between thick and thin strokes is very marked, eg:

ABCabcd

fat matter	printer's slang for copy which can be set quickly because it includes a lot of space (eg: dialogue in novels); opposite of 'lean matter'
fax	slang for electronically transmitted images produced by scanning original (from 'facsimile')

feature card index   see 'peek-a-boo card index'

feedback   in electronic transmission, return of some part of output of system to input, positive feedback re-inforcing input, negative feedback reducing it; in information sciences generally, negative feedback forms essential element of self-correcting control systems

feet (type)   that part of piece of type upon which it stands (see 'type')

feint lines   typical product of 'run-through work' (qv): horizontal lines (customarily light blue) ruled on sheets which are made up as manuscript books and account books

fibre optics   technique of transmitting image through flexible bundle of fine, tubular fibres, allowing subjects in narrow confines to be examined and/or photographed by means of device called an 'endoscope'

field area/size   in cinefilm and TV, area viewed by camera from any given position:

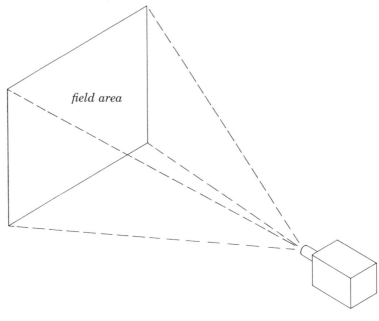

field area

field guide   specially printed sheet on which 'zooming' and 'panning' movements are planned in film animation

figure (type)   term commonly used by printers and typefounders for 'numeral'

figure (in book)	traditional term for line illustration incorporated within text pages of book, as distinct from 'plate' (qv); often abbreviated as 'fig' (pl: 'figs')
filling-in	printing fault resulting in filling in of 'counters' (qv) of type and of fine white dots in halftones
film-advance	in photocomposition, amount by which sensitive material in 'photounit' (qv) is advanced to achieve required distance between lines of output
film animation	in cinefilm and TV, shooting of separate film frames in sequence to produce illusion of movement; any shot which is not achieved by conventional photography at constant camera speed will involve some measure of film animation, though most common uses are for cartoons and title/credit sequences
film assembly	in photolithography, assembly of film negatives or positives in position for making printing plates
film clip	short length of cinefilm, especially from final version of movie
film sizes	commonly available sizes of film for use in still cameras are:

110	16mm film width, perforated one side; twelve or twenty exposures 13 × 17mm in cartridge
126	35mm film width, perforated one side; twelve or twenty exposures 26 × 26mm in cartridge
135	35mm film width, perforated both sides; forty or seventy-two exposures 18 × 24mm in cassette, twelve, twenty or thirty-six exposures 24 × 36mm in cassette
120	62mm film width, in unperforated roll with backing paper; fifteen exposures 45 × 60mm, twelve exposures 60 × 60mm, ten exposures 60 × 70mm, eight exposures 60 × 90mm
220	62mm film width, in unperforated roll without backing paper; same range of image sizes as for 120, but with double number of exposures in each

sheet film comes in large variety of sizes of which common traditional ones are:

quarter-plate 83 × 108mm (3¼ × 4¾in)*
halfplate 121 × 165mm (4¾ × 6½in)*

63

whole-plate 165 × 216mm (6½ × 8½in)*
203 × 254mm (8 × 10in)
102 × 127mm (4 × 5in)
* now obsolescent and being replaced by 'A' sizes

film speed	all photographic film – including cinefilm – has a speed rating (the higher the number, the faster the film) from which is calculated exposure; two matching standards, ASA and DIN, are used, and these are shown on calibration scales of exposure meters
film strip (matrix)	in photocomposition, 'image-carrier' (qv) in form of film strip
filmograph	in film animation; technique whereby movements of rostrum camera and table create effect of animation from artwork and still photographs
filmsetting	used as synonym for 'photocomposition' (qv) but not so suitable as generic term since it implies setting only on film, for which specific function it is best reserved
filter	in photography, sheet of glass, plastic or gelatin placed between subject and lens of camera, which modifies or eliminates certain colour from emulsion of film
filter factor	adjustment which must be made in photographic exposure when filter is used
fine screen	any 'halftone screen' (qv) of 100 lines to the inch (40 lines to the centimetre) or finer
finial letter	special sort in some typefaces intended for use only at end of word or line; see 'swash letter'
finish	treatment of paper surface to give final effect, during manufacture or subsequently
finished art	same as 'artwork' (qv)
finished rough	nonsense term for 'presentation visual' (qv)
firmware	computer programs embodied in components which cannot themselves be altered by user but may be removed and replaced
first angle projection	see 'multiview projections'

fish-eye lens	one which has an extremely wide angle (about 150° – 180°) producing very distorted circular image:

fist	printer's slang for index mark in form of pointing hand:

fit-up halftones	in letterpress, two or more halftone plates which are made separately but fitted up together in mounting, as distinct from 'stripped-up halftones' which are combined at negative stage and made up as one plate
fix, fixer	chemical solution used to make images on photographic film and prints permanent; in slang use, same as 'hypo'
fixed word spacing	typesetting mode in which word spaces are all standard, any extra space being left at end of line, same as 'even word spacing'; this book is set to fixed word spacing throughout
flag (of newspaper)	same as 'nameplate' (qv)
flange	below-type-height edge of letterpress halftone plate, through which it is secured to mount by pins; now often unnecessary as plates are adhesive mounted
flash-harry	derogatory term applied by some graphic designers to their more imaginative colleagues
flat	in photolitho platemaking, special opaque base from which 'windows' are cut for insertion of negative material, whole assembly forming composite used to print down image on albumen plate

flat-bed cylinder press	printing machine using impression cylinder as distinct from 'platen press' (qv) and having flat printing surface as distinct from 'rotary press' (qv)
flat-bed plotter	computer output device consisting of flat drawing table traversed by writing-tool assembly which produces drawings on paper or film to high standard of accuracy
flat-tint halftone	matching halftone with flat tint to print under it in separate colour
fleuron	see 'printer's flower'
flexography	relief printing process using curved plates of rubber or soft plastic; used mostly for packaging and paper bags
flip box	same as 'flop-over box' (qv)
flippy, flippy-floppy	double-sided version of 'floppy disc' (qv)
floating accent	in typesetting, separate accent mark which can be 'floated' over suitable lower-case character (known as 'piece accent' in US)
floating bar graph	one in which variables occur at either end of bar:

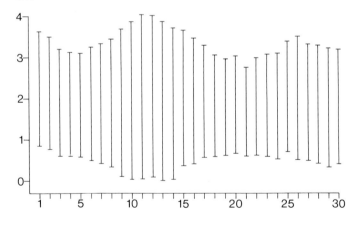

flong	material used for making moulds from type matter, from which stereos (qv) are cast; also called 'matrix' or 'mat'
flop	in photomechanical reproduction, reversing an image left-to-right, whether by accident or intent

flop-over box, flop box	in film animation, device by means of which still image appears to rotate horizontally or vertically:

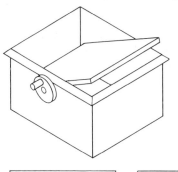

floppy disc	magnetic disc in flexible plastic, about same size as 45 rpm single record, used as alternative to magnetic tape in many photocomposition systems; also known as 'diskette'
floret	see 'printer's flower'
flowchart	diagram to show flow of process, activity or sequence of events; those used in data processing are of two types, systems flowcharts and program flowcharts:

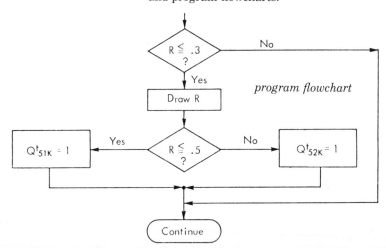

flowcharting symbols   those most commonly used in data processing are:

system flowcharting:

process

manual
operation

auxiliary
operation

merge

extract

collate

sort

display

manual
input

general
input/output

connector

annotation

document

punched
card

punched
paper tape

magnetic
tape

drum

disk

additional symbols for program flowcharting:

preparation

subroutine

decision

keying

terminal

off-page
connector

flower   see 'printer's flower'

flowline map   one in which route of traffic flow is shown by line and rate of flow
                        by varying thickness of that line, thus:

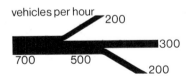

flush left/right   same as 'ranged left/right' (qv)

68

flush mount	letterpress halftone plate with 'flange' (qv) removed to fit up close to type matter or another plate
fly-fold	same as '4 page fold' (see 'folding methods')
fly leaf	that part of 'endpaper' (qv) at front of book which is glued to first text leaf
focal depth	see 'depth of focus'
focal length	notional measurement from camera lens to point at which distant image is in sharp focus, marked on lens by an 'f' followed by measurements from centre of lens to film when set at 'infinity', eg: 'f = 50mm':

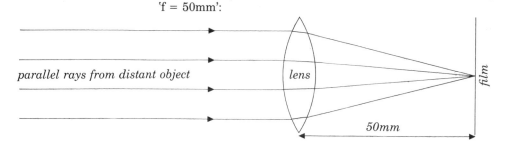

parallel rays from distant object　　*lens*　　*film*

50mm

lenses are classified according to focal length and maximum 'aperture' (qv), and fall into general categories of short focus, standard and long focus:

image from whole negative through short focus lens

image from whole negative through long focus lens

fog	in photography, grey tone over whole or part of film or paper caused by accidental exposure to light during processing
foil	metallic mixture used in 'blocking' (qv); also, paper coated with metallic leaf or powder, used in boxmaking
fold-out	leaf of book extending beyond page width, so that it must be folded one or more times; also called 'throw-out' or 'pull-out':

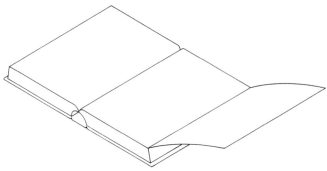

fold-to-paper	folding printed section (signature) by matching edges of sheet
fold-to-print	folding printed section (signature) matching print matter (usually page numbers); more accurate than 'fold-to-paper'
folder	piece of print which is folded but not bound; also – confusingly – container for loose items of print
folding methods	standard patterns of paper folding in print are:

single fold   *double (gate) fold*   *double (concertina) fold*

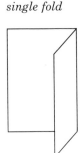 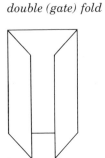 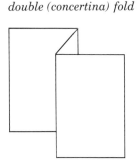

continuous fold (concertina) *parallel fold* *right angle fold*

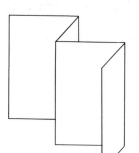
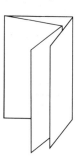

foliation (of book)	numbering leaves rather than pages, as distinct from 'pagination'
folio	cut or folded sheet which is half of basic sheet size; also used as synonym for 'page number'
follow copy	instruction to printer on manuscript or proof to set copy exactly as given, despite apparent errors
foot	bottom of book (qv); also known as 'tail'
foot margin	see 'page'
foredge, fore-edge	edge of book opposite back or spine (see also 'book')
foredge margin	see 'page'
format	dimensions of trimmed sheet, page or book; also general term for size, style and treatment
formatting	setting up command codes for computer-aided photocomposition, based on typographic mark-up
forme (form in US)	type matter, blocks and spacing material locked up in 'chase' (qv) as complete letterpress printing unit; by extension, complete lithographic plate for printing one side of sheet
FORTRAN	see 'computer languages'
forwarding	in book production, originally those operations from sewing to application of cover, now taken to incl'

fortyeight sheet	poster size 120 × 480in (305 × 1220cm)
founder's/foundry type	type cast in very hard metal by type founders for use in hand composition, as distinct from type cast in machine composition for one-job-only use
fount (spelled font in US and so pronounced in UK)	set of characters of one size of typeface, usually comprising lower case, capitals, small capitals, ligatures, numerals (figures), punctuation marks, reference marks, signs and spaces; italic and bold founts are usually smaller than roman founts, omitting, for example, small caps
fountain	on offset-litho machines, reservoir for supply of fountain solution (water, acid and gum) to dampening rollers; may also, confusingly, refer to 'ink duct' (qv), especially in US
four-colour process	full-colour printing from plates produced by photographic separation into subtractive primary colours (cyan, magenta, yellow) and black
free footage	in film animation, any shot which involves only camera or panning table movements with no need for additional drawn animation
free line-fall	same as 'ragged right' (qv); more common in US
freeze-frame	in cinefilm and TV, special optical effect in which movement is stopped at certain point in action; also called 'still-frame' in TV
french curves	flat plastic shapes with combinations of curves, used for tracing:

french fold	right angle fold when used for invitations or similar items of print in order to have print on inside and outside with only one printing
sewing (of book)	method using only thread, with no cord or tape support

Fresnel lens	in photography, special condenser lens used on spotlight to concentrate light beam or in viewing screen to assist focussing
front lay edge	see 'lay edges'
front matter (of book)	same as 'prelims' (qv); more common in US
front projection	in cinefilm, TV and still photography, taken to mean projection of images on two-way mirror interposed between camera and main subject:

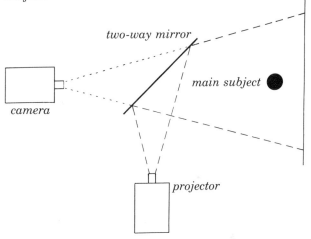

frontispiece, frontis	illustration on preliminary page of book, usually facing title page
fudge	stop-press matter in newspaper contained within 'fudge-box' on printing press
fugitive ink	one which fades or changes colour on exposure to light, as distinct from 'light-fast' or 'permanent' ink
full-faced type	US synonym for 'titling' (qv)
full-out	instruction to printer to set line or lines of type without indentation
full point	printer's term for 'full stop' or 'period'
full-sized fraction	one made up from full-sized numerals, thus: 1/3
furnish	mixture of materials used in making of paper

73

| furniture | in letterpress, material used to take up space around type and blocks before locking up forme for printing |

G

| galley | metal tray used to hold composed type before it is made up in page |

| galley proof | rough proof, in long strip, of composed type before it is made up in page; sometimes called 'slip proof' |

| galley slave | slang term for 'compositor' (archaic, but too good to leave out) |

| gang-ups | several print jobs run off on same sheet of paper, which is then cut up into individual pieces |

| garland | sometimes used to describe book of poems or prose extracts |

| gate-fold | see 'folding methods' |

| gathering | arranging sheets or sections in correct order so as to make up book: |

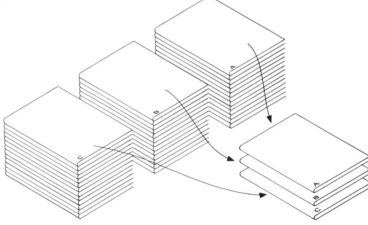

sections (signatures) gathered in reverse order according to signature marks at foot of first page of each section

| ⁓tric figures | see 'angles', 'quadrilaterals', 'regular polygons' and 'regular solids' |

geometric sans-serif	one constructed of geometric shapes, with even line thickness and usually having single storey 'a' and 'g':

ABCDEFGHIJK abcdefghijk

gestalt	German for 'configuration'; Gestalt School of psychology relates to ways in which images are perceived and understood
gigo, GIGO	initials of 'garbage in – garbage out', name given to principle which holds that no computer program can produce good output from bad input
glassine	transparent, glazed paper used for wrappings and window envelopes
glyphic (of typeface)	one which suggests origin in chiselled, rather than calligraphic, model
g/m^2	abbreviation for 'grammes per square metre'; method of denoting substance of paper by weight, now standard in most of Europe including UK; this weight factor is known as 'grammage'
golden section	harmonious proportion arising from division of any line A-C at point B so that AB is to AC as BC is to AB; this ratio (1 : 1.618) provides dimensions of 'golden rectangle':

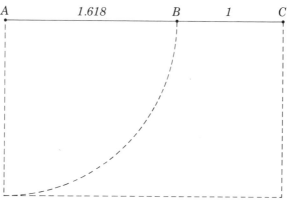

goldenrod	opaque, pre-ruled paper used for litho 'flat' (qv)
golf-ball	colloquial name for spherical typing head of IBM 72 typewriter and its derivatives

gothic	same as 'black letter' (qv), but in US refers to sans-serif typefaces, particularly of nineteenth century vintage; best avoided except as part of name of typeface
gouache	opaque, gum-based paint soluble in water; particularly suitable for use in presentation visuals and artwork for reproduction
grain (of film)	in photography, clumps of minute silver grains which form image in film emulsion; may become visible as speckle pattern due to excessive enlargement
grain (of paper)	see 'machine direction'
grammage	see 'g/m^2'
grammes per square metre	see 'g/m^2'
graph	see 'coordinate graph', 'bar graph', 'logarithmic graph', 'pie graph', 'scatter graph' and 'star graph'; for another meaning, see 'graph theory' below
graph plotter	see 'drum plotter' and 'flat-bed plotter'
graph theory	one dealing with geometric figures (graphs), consisting of points (vertices) and lines (edges), used to express relations and connexions; see also 'network diagram'
graphic/graphical display terminal	electronic device used in computer-aided photocomposition and other graphic visualizing tasks
graphic (of typeface)	one which suggests origin in drawn, rather than written, model:

ABCDEF
claim as valid

graticule	cross-line grid laid over image so as to provide key to features within in (eg: lines of longitude and latitude on maps)
grave accent	see 'accented (diacritical) signs'
gravure	same as 'photogravure' (qv)

Greek alphabet	characters in Greek alphabet are:			
	Αα *alpha*	Ηη *eta*	Νν *nu*	Ττ *tau*
	Ββ *beta*	Θθ *theta*	Ξξ *xi/si*	Υυ *upsilon*
	Γγ *gamma*	Ιι *iota*	Οο *omicron*	Φφ *phi*
	Δδ *delta*	Κκ *kappa*	Ππ *pi*	Χχ *chi*
	Εε *epsilon*	Λλ *lambda*	Ρρ *rho*	Ψψ *psi*
	Ζζ *zeta*	Μμ *mu*	Σσς *sigma*	Ωω *omega*

grey scale   one used in photomechanical reproduction to check correct exposure and development time

grid (matrix)   in photocomposition, an 'image-carrier' (qv) in grid form

gripper edge   edge of sheet which is held by mechanical grippers when being fed into printing press, that is, leading or front edge; sometimes called 'front lay edge'

gripper margin   that margin which has to be allowed for on sheet so that it can be gripped without affecting area of job when trimmed

grotesque   kind of sans-serif typeface dating from mid-19th century (also known as 'gothic' in US), as distinguished from 'humanist sans-serif' (qv) and 'geometric sans-serif' (qv):

gsm   earlier, now incorrect, form of 'g/m^2' (qv)

guarding   method of attaching single leaf to section of book or periodical, as more secure alternative to 'tipping in/on' (qv):

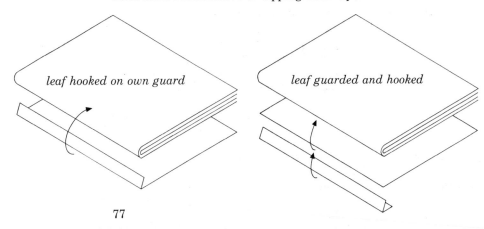

leaf hooked on own guard   *leaf guarded and hooked*

guides	see 'lays'
guillemets	French quotation marks « thus »; also used in some German texts
gutter	space between pages, including allowance for trim, when imposed in forme (see 'imposition'); sometimes wrongly used to describe channel between two columns of type

H & J, H/J	initials of 'hyphenation and justification'; see 'end-of-line decisions',
hachures	in some maps, lines drawn down slopes in direction of steepest gradients, placed closer together where slope is steeper
hairline	finest printable line, as used for serifs in 'modern-face' (qv)
hairspace	in hand composition, thinnest available space, either ½pt or 1pt in width; used mainly for letter spacing
halation	in photography, halo effect produced by bright light source contrasting with darker surround or silhouette:

half-sheet work	form of imposition in which section is made from one half of whole sheet so that two identical sections are made from each half (see also 'work-and-turn' and 'work-and-tumble')
half-title	right-hand page preceding title page of book, containing title only

halftone	continuous tone subject, whether original or converted for reproduction, in contrast to line subject
halftone process	photomechanical reproduction of continuous-tone originals by means of technique which converts image into minute graded dots giving appearance of continuous tone, achieved by photographing original through glass or film screen containing pattern of fine crossed lines which split image into white or black dots according to variation of dark and light tones in original:

standard ruling for halftone screens are:

rulings per inch		50	65	85	100	120	133	150	175	200
rulings per centimetre		20	26	30	40	48	54	60	70	80

half-up	artwork prepared one-and-a-half times reproduced size, so as to ensure fine detail and accuracy
hand-sorted punched card	same as 'edge-notched card' (qv)
hanging indent	in typesetting, indenting all lines in paragraph except first one; also known as 'reverse indent'
hanging punctuation	punctuation marks set outside type measure as stylistic refinement
hard-backed book	one with stiff board cover
hard copy	typed duplicate produced by computer-controlled photocomposing system, to check accuracy of input before setting
hard (paper)	in photography, one giving high contrast image
hardware	used by computer makers and users to describe equipment itself, as distinct from programs and operating procedures (known as 'software')
hard-wired	in photocomposition, those functions which are incorporated so that they cannot be re-programmed except by altering wiring of machine
Hart's Rules	publication setting out rules for compositors and printer readers in connexion with spelling, hyphenation, abbreviation, punctuation, etc (see Bibliography)
head	top edge of book (qv)
head bolt	thickening of sheet at last (head) fold before trimming:

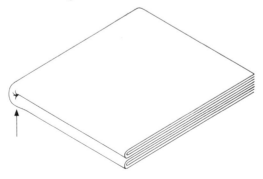

heat-set inks   those designed for quick-drying by application of heat, which vaporises oil content and allows residue to harden more speedily

heavy (type)   sometimes used instead of 'bold' (qv) to denote typeface variant

hectography   process of printing limited number of copies by means of gelatin plate and special ink

height-to-paper   same as 'type-height' (qv)

helix   'locus' (qv) of point which moves round circumference of cylinder or cone and axially at same time, with ratio of two movements constant, as in corkscrew:

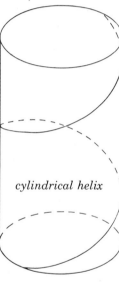
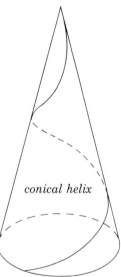

cylindrical helix   *conical helix*

heuristics   study of problem-solving by means of trial and error, involving successive evaluations at each step towards final solution; as distinct from 'algorithmics' (qv)

hexagram   figure formed by two intersecting equilateral triangles:

81

hickie, hickey	in printing, speck of dust, bit of loose ink or other intrusive matter which has become stuck to type matter plate or offset blanket and shows up as haloed spot
hieratic script	later, abridged form of hieroglyphic writing
hieroglyph	Greek for 'holy carving'; used especially to describe ancient Egyptian inscriptions and writings; basically pictogrammatic, though ideograms and phonograms were also used
high gloss ink	one having 'vehicle' (qv) so composed that ink does not penetrate deeply into paper and so has varnished appearance
high key	photographic image in which, by lighting and/or processing, most of tones are very light:

highlight halftone	same as 'drop-out halftone' (qv)
histogram	'coordinate graph' (qv) in which frequency percentage is plotted as ordinate and varying quantity as abscissa, usually as 'bar graph'
holding line	US term for 'keyline' (qv)
hologram/holograph image	one which gives three-dimensional illusion without use of camera: laser beam (known as 'coherent light') is split so that diffraction patterns are produced on photographic film; these reconstitute image of subject when illuminated by light from similar laser
holograph (publishing)	manuscript wholly written in author's own hand
hooking	see 'guarding'
hot metal composition	any typeset matter originating in hot metal casting: Monotype,

hot press lettering	depositing metal foil image from type, by means of heat and pressure, onto board; used for shop display cards, TV captions, etc
house corrections	proof corrections of printer's errors, made by printer's reader and shown on 'master proof' (qv); rectified at printer's expense
house style	imposed rules of design by which commercial, professional, charitable or state-supported body establishes consistency, coherence and recognizability in its publicity, promotion, stationery, packaging and distribution; also known as 'corporate identity'; may also refer to sets of rules for printers, as 'Hart's Rules' (qv)
h/t	abbreviation for 'halftone' (qv)
hue	means of distinguishing one colour from another by measuring predominating wavelengths of coloured substances
humanist	applied to typefaces generally, distinguishes those roman and venetian designs based on revived carolingian scripts used by Italian Renaissance scholars in 15th century
humanist sans-serif	one based on proportions of roman and venetian typefaces, usually having two-storey 'a' and 'g':

TASTES changed

hyphenation	splitting one word or compounding two or more words by use of hyphen; used rather inaccurately to describe word-breaking at end of line of type
hyperbola	'locus' (qv) of point which moves so that ratio of its distances from fixed point and from fixed straight line is constant and greater than one; see also 'conic sections'
hyperfocal distance	in photography, distance from camera lens to nearest object which is acceptably sharp when focussed on infinity
hypo	slang for sodium hyposulphate, wrongly supposed to be fixing solution for photographic film and paper (it is, in fact, sodium thiosulphate)

I

ibid — abbreviation for *ibidem*, Latin for 'in the same place'; used in footnotes to refer to book, chapter or passage already referred to

ICOGRADA — initials of International Council of Graphic Design Associations, founded 1963 to act as talking shop for professional, educational and technical aspects of graphic design

ideal format — in photography, increasingly popular negative size of 60 × 70mm, devised to satisfy those wanting rectangular format larger than, and not so elongated as, 35mm format (24 × 36mm)

idem — Latin for '(by) the same'; used in footnotes

ideogram/graph — character which symbolizes an idea by representing associated object but does not express sounds of its name; many Chinese characters are ideograms

imitation art — cheaper substitute for art paper, in which clay content is added during paper-making instead of being laid on subsequently

ie — initials of *id est*, Latin for 'that is'

idiot tape — see 'unjustified tape'

IIP — initials of 'Institute of Incorporated Photographers'; body representing those practising professionally as photographers in UK

image carrier — useful term covering those components of photocomposition systems (either disc, grid, drum or film strip) having same function as set of type matrices in machine composition; also called 'image master'

impose — to arrange type and other print matter in pages and lock up as forme for printing

imposed proof — proof taken from forme; also called 'sheet proof'

imposition — arrangement of pages to printed on sheet in unit called 'forme' (qv) so that they will be in correct sequence when folded to form section (signature); simplest imposition is for 4 pages:

 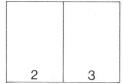

and 16 page imposition is typical:

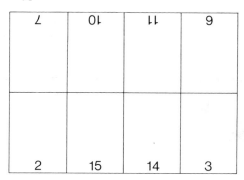

other common impositions are for 8 pages and 32 pages, though 12, 24 and 32 pages are also feasible; imposition plans are vital planning tools since they show instantly which pages are on same side of sheet, how to arrange colour economically and how to re-arrange imposition if particular colour sequence is required (see also 'work and tumble', 'work and turn' and 'work and twist')

impossible triangle representation of object which cannot exist in reality, devised by psychologists LS and R Penrose in 1958:

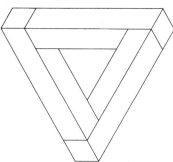

impression any printed copy made from type matter or plates, and physical action which produces it; also, by extension, whole print run (used in connexion with number of copies printed)

impression cylinder	that part of 'cylinder press' (qv) which receives paper, takes it into contact with inked type matter or plate and makes impression
imprint (publisher's)	publisher's name printed on title page of book
imprint (printer's)	printer's name, usually shown inconspicuously on reverse of title page or at foot of last page
imprint page	reverse of title page of book, used for information about copyright conditions, printing history and printer; also called 'biblio' page
in-betweens	in film animation, those drawings (often made by another hand) which fill in movement between 'extremes' (qv)
in-camera process	one in which development of image takes place within camera, as in Polaroid and Kodak Instant Picture cameras
increment	see 'line increment'
incunabulum (pl: incunabula)	Latin for 'from the cradle'; used to describe an early book, especially one printed before 1501
indent	to leave blank space at beginning of line of type, usually first line of paragraph
index	alphabetical list of subjects dealt with in book, with relevant page numbers; but see also 'step', 'tab' and 'thumb' index
index board	materials with high machine finish, produced in range of tints for use in card index systems
indirect letterpress	same as 'letterset' (qv)
inferior figure/letter	small character set to appear below level of normal characters of typeface; eg: H_2SO_4
information theory	extension of 'communication theory' (qv) from mathematics into other, less specific fields of science, including communication
infra-red	near visible waves in 'electromagnetic spectrum' (qv) which can show on some photographic materials
in-house/in-plant print	work executed by organization whose main business is not printing but which has its own printing plant

in pro	abbreviation of 'in proportion', used when giving instructions to reduce or enlarge originals in proportion to one another
injection-moulding	injecting liquefied plastics material into space between matched moulds, thus:

material injected here

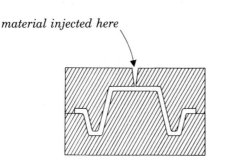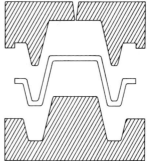

ink duct	ink reservoir on printing machine from which supply of ink is regulated; sometimes referred to (especially in US) as 'ink fountain'; see also 'split duct/fountain' and 'fountain'
ink duplicating	simple planographic printing process for up to 1,000 copies, using negative stencil master produced by drawing or typing; also known as 'mimeography', from trade name 'Mimeograph'
ink-jet printer	computer output device using high speed ink jets to make image
ink squash	printing characteristic, particularly of letterpress, in which ink spreads beyond outline of impression surface
inking roller	that part of printing machine used to transfer ink from ink supply to printing surface
inner forme	one which includes pages forming innermost spread of folded section
input	expression used in computer-controlled operations to describe any information (data) to be processed
inserting	adding separately printed piece into book or periodical after binding
insetting	placing one unit of book or periodical into another; 'insetted work'

is so called to distinguish it from gathered work (see 'gathering'):

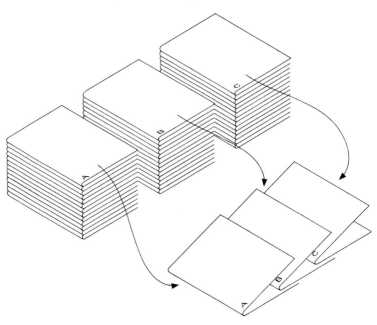

intaglio

general description for those printing processes (eg: photogravure) in which inked image is in etched or engraved recesses below surface of printing plate

interface

useful jargon for place where interaction occurs between two systems or processes, or between human and machine

interlay

prepared paper inserted between letterpress printing plate and its mount to build up strength of tone in darker areas and decrease it in lighter areas

interleaving

to place unprinted sheets between printed sheets as they come off press, to prevent 'set-off' (qv); known as 'slip-sheeting' in US

interlinear spacing

in photocomposition, equivalent of 'leading'

international paper sizes

see 'A, B and C Series'

international phonetic alphabet	1) agreed code for spelling out letters of words over telephone:

A	Alfa	J	Julia	S	Sierra
B	Bravo	K	Kilo	T	Tango
C	Charlie	L	Lima	U	Uniform
D	Delta	M	Mike	V	Victor
E	Echo	N	November	W	Whisky
F	Foxtrot	O	Oscar	X	X-ray
G	Golf	P	Papa	Y	Yankee
H	Hotel	Q	Quebec	Z	Zulu
I	India	R	Romeo		

2) special type characters (not properly an alphabet) designed to represent accurately all speech sounds, eg:

ˈɪnglɪʃ prənʌnsɪ ˈeɪʃn

internegative, interneg — intermediate stage between positive original (opaque or transparent) and print

interrogating typewriter — 'teleprinter' (qv) used for direct transmission of data from computer to distant terminal and vice-versa

Intertype — type composing machine which produces line of type (slug) in one piece, similar to Linotype

inverted commas — pair of commas inverted thus " to signify opening of quotation; also known as 'turned commas' (but note that typeface in this work uses commas reversed left-to-right, not inverted)

involute — 'locus' (qv) of point fixed on line which rolls, without slipping, around polygon:

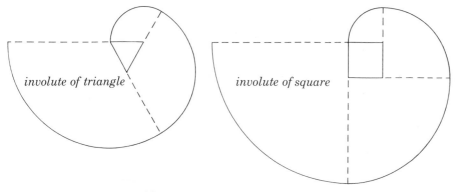

involute of triangle   *involute of square*

Ionic	range of typefaces dating from mid-19th century, slab-seriffed with slight bracketing, much used in newspaper work
iph	initials of 'impressions per hour'; measure of rate of printing machine
iris (of camera)	usual form of diaphragm which controls 'aperture' (qv)
ISBN	initials of 'International Standard Book Number', ten-digit number allocated to each publisher book, with separate number for each edition; first part of number is group identifier (ie: country or group of countries), second part is publisher identifier, third part is title identifier and last part is single check digit
iso-	prefix meaning 'same' (as in 'isometric')
ISO	initials of 'International Standards Organization', body based in Switzerland who publish many Standards and Recommendations, including 'A, B and C Series' of paper and envelope sizes (qv), 'film speed' ratings (qv) and an ever-increasing number relating to publishing (see Bibliography)
isometric projection	'axonometric projection' (qv) in which axes are arranged at 120° to each other and all dimensions along axes are in same scale ratio
Isotype	acronym for 'International System of Typographical Picture Education', system of pictorial graph-making pioneered by Otto Neurath in Vienna from 1924
italic	originally, typeface of cursive character based on chancery italic (ie: Italian) handwriting; now used for any face with characters which incline noticeably to right, though some of these are more properly called 'sloped roman':

specialized **documents**

true italic *sloped roman*

ivory board	high-grade white board of even finish with clear, translucent look-through, used mainly for business and greeting cards

J

jet printing   see 'ink-jet printing'

jim-dash   short rule between newspaper items

jobbing printer   one who takes on various sorts of work and is not tied to one particular kind (called 'job shop' in US)

jogging   aligning edges of stack of paper sheets by using vibration

joystick (VDT)   attachment to VDT which permits operator to change or adapt images on screen:

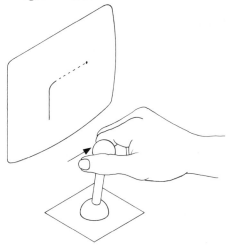

jump   carry over portion of newspaper or periodical feature from one page to another, hence 'jump-line'

jump-cut   in cinefilm and TV, any cut between two takes which jars on the eyes; may be intentional or just bad camerawork and editing

justified (of type)   lines of type set so as to fill 'measure' (qv); less accurately, but usefully, lines of type that range visually on both sides

K

keep down	instruction to compositor: keep type in lower-case (newspaper term)
keep in	instruction to compositor: use narrow word spaces
keep standing	instruction to printer to keep type matter ready for possible reprinting
keep out	instruction to compositor: use wide word spaces (same as 'drive out')
keep up	instruction to printer: keep type in caps (newspaper term)
kern	part of piece of type sticking out to one side of body so that it overlaps onto adjacent piece:

 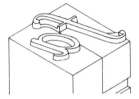

kerning	applied to type which kerns, now used in photocomposition to describe a backspacing technique whereby one character may be tucked into another, thus: Ta, WA; also applied to dubious practice of compressing copy to fit line by 'minus' or abnormally close letter-spacing
key plate	in colour printing, that plate which is to print first, providing key for registering subsequent colours (also called 'first colour down')
keys	in film animation, same as 'extremes' (qv)
keyboarding	in machine- and photocomposition, first operation of typing in copy to be set; until advent of photocomposition, operator was known as 'compositor' (US: 'typographer'), but is now increasingly described as 'keyboard operator' or even 'keyboardist', especially when producing 'unjustified tape' (qv)
keyline	outline drawn on artwork to indicate area of solid or position of halftone image; also called 'holding line'

92

keyword index, keyword-from-title index	one using significant word or words in title of written work by which it may be identified for retrieval, especially from computer-operated memory store; keywords may be shown in context of rest of title (KWIC) or outside it (KWOC)
kicker	line of type above or below title of newspaper or periodical feature
kill	delete unwanted copy or 'dis' unwanted type matter
kiss impression	in letterpress, ideal impression whereby image is rich and well inked but paper shows no sign of embossing effect
kraft paper	tough, brown paper used for wrapping
KWIC/KWOC indexes	initials of 'keyword-in-context index' and 'keyword-out-of-context' (see 'keyword index')

L

lacuna	missing portion of text resulting from damage to manuscript or book
laid paper	uncoated paper that shows faint pattern of ribbed lines – 'laid' lines and 'chain' lines – when looked at through light and slight corrugations on one side (known as 'wire-side'), caused during making
Lambert's projections	see 'cylindrical projections' and 'zenithal projections'
laminate	to apply transparent plastic film to sheet of paper or board, giving hard, glossy surface; also used as noun to describe such products
landscape format	describes proportion of film, photoprint, artwork or any piece of print matter in which height is appreciably shorter than width
lap	small overlap allowed when two printed colours abut, so as to prevent risk of any gap resulting from slight lack of register
large face	larger of two sizes available on same body of typeface
Lasercomp	trade name for photocomposition system involving use of laser beam

latent image	in photography, any image capable of being developed chemically
Latin (of typefaces)	in general, all typefaces derived from western European letterforms, as distinct from, say, Arabic or Hebrew; more specifically (and confusingly), those typefaces having 'wedge-serifs' (qv)
lay edges	those edges of sheet which are presented to side 'lays' of printing machine; front edge is usually called 'gripper edge' (qv) though 'front lay edge' is equally correct
lays	on printing machines, devices at front and side to which paper is fed before processing (printing, folding, stamping, perforating, etc); more commonly known in US as 'guides'
layout	plan designed to show how printed result is to be obtained and give some idea of how it would look
layout grid	pre-printed sheet with lines showing basic pattern to be followed in designing layouts or preparing paste-up artwork
LCD	initials of 'liquid crystal display': type of electronic display for editing terminals, pocket calculators and the like, in form of black or silver characters on coloured or near-white ground
lead (pron: led)	thin strip of metal used to separate lines of type; made in standard thicknesses of 1pt, 1½pt, 2pt, 3pt, 6pt and 12pt
leader (pron: leeder)	1) in photography and cinefilm, blank film at beginning and end of roll or reel, used for threading to take-up spool 2) in printing, line of dots, thus.........used to take eye along line of type from one item to another
leaf	two backing pages of book
LED	initials of 'light emitting diode': electronic display having same function as 'LCD' above, but with red characters on dark ground
legend	rather archaic synonym of 'caption' (qv)
lens flare	in photography, tendency of camera lens to scatter light, especially from intense light source
lens-oriented	jargon adjective applied to areas of practice or study which include still photography, cinefilm and TV

letter assembly	catch-all term with same connotation as 'character assembly' (qv), but less useful because less inclusive
letter fit	in type design, way in which characters are arranged to fit harmoniously with one another; better term would be 'character fit'
letterpress	printing process in which impression is taken from raised surfaces of type matter or blocks; also called 'relief' or 'typographic' process:

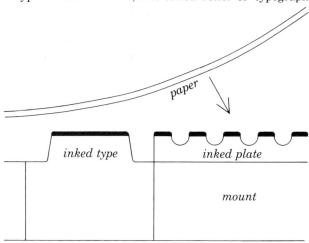

letterpress book	used by some to describe book which is printed (by whatever process) as distinct from 'stationery book'
letterset	rotary letterpress which transfers image from wraparound plate of offset cylinder, as with offset-litho (contraction of 'letterpress-offset')
letter-spacing	inserting spaces between letters within word, as distinct from 'word-spacing' (qv): letter-space
lhp	abbreviation of 'left-hand page'
library binding	one of strength and durability suited to frequent handling of book over long period
library shot	in cinefilm and TV, one from existing source, not specially taken
lifting	same as 'picking' (qv)

ligature	two or three characters joined together as one (or more precisely the visible link joining them), eg:

light-fast ink	one which does not fade appreciably when exposed to light for long periods, as distinct from 'fugitive' ink
light pen (VDT)	mobile, highly sensitive photoelectric attachment resembling pen, used with some VDTs to call up images from computer store by passing 'pen' over surface of screen; can also be used to change or adapt them:

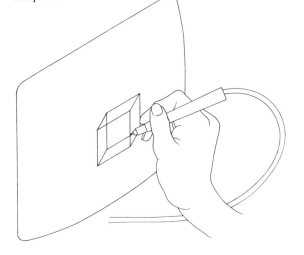

limp binding	one with flexible cover made of paper, cloth or plastic; usually called 'soft binding' or 'soft cover' in US
line-and-halftone plate	line and halftone images combined on one plate; known in US as 'combination plate' or 'combo'
line feed	amount, measured in points or parts of point, by which direct impression and photocomposition machines advance paper or film from line to line; also known as 'film feed'
line block	one which produces line result (ie: not halftone); called 'linecut' or 'line engraving' in US

line caster	typesetting machine which casts type as one whole line (slug) as against single-character caster
line conversion	transforming halftone original into line image by eliminating all middle tones; sometimes called 'drop-out' (but see 'drop-out halftone')
line-endless tape	same as 'unjustified tape' (qv) and 'idiot tape'; often, (most confusingly) shortened to 'endless tape'
line gauge	same as 'type scale' (qv)
line graph	see 'coordinate graph'
line increment	in typesetting, smallest amount by which basic line interval may be increased; in hot metal typesetting this is ½ 'point' (qv) but in photocomposition it may be as little as one-eighteenth of a point
line interval	vertical distance between base line of one line of type to base line of next; basic line interval corresponds to 'body size' of metal type but this phrase has no relevance for photocomposition and direct impression methods
line original	one that is intended for line reproduction
line printer	computer output device, in form of drum, chain or CRT printer, which prints out whole line of characters at once, at speeds of 500–2,000 lpm (lines per minute); may be used in photocomposition to produce 'hard copy' for proof-reading
linen tester	form of magnifying glass especially suited to examining dot-patterns of halftone reproductions in detail
– line type	method of size measurement for wooden type, one 'line' being 12 points
lining figures	set of type numerals which line up with capitals thus: 1234567890 as distinct from 'old style figures' (qv); sometimes known as 'ranging figures'
lining-up table	one with surface illuminated from below and with grid lines and/or moving scales superimposed, used to check accuracy of film positives and negatives, and back-up and register of proofs

Linofilm	trade name for photocomposition system of Linotype Paul (UK) and Mergenthaler (US)
Linotron	trade name for high speed photocomposing system of Linotype Paul (UK) and Mergenthaler (US)
Linotype	type composing machine which produces a line of type (slug) in one piece, similar to Intertype
linting	in offset lithography, accumulation of loose bits of uncoated paper on surface of blanket cylinder, affecting print quality
lip-sync	in cinefilm and TV, matching lip movements of speaker on film to sound recording of voice
literal	spelling error due to wrong, or omitted, letter in typesetting; known as 'typo' (typographic error) in US
literary-minded	derogatory term applied by some graphic designers to others who show concern for such factors as readability
lith film	one that gives high definition and high contrast, cutting out middle tones, used for photomechanical reproduction
lithography (abb: litho)	'planographic' (qv) printing process (the commercial form of which is photolithography) in which surface of stone or metal is treated with chemicals so that some portions accept ink and some reject it:

rubber blanket

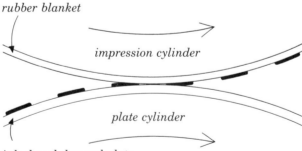

impression cylinder

plate cylinder

inked and damped plate

live matter (typesetting)	set matter intended for use, as distinct from 'dead matter'
loading (of paper)	substance added to pulp of paper to improve opacity and allow high finish (eg: china clay)

loc cit	abbreviation for *loco citato,* Latin for 'in the place cited'; used in footnotes
logarithmic graph	coordinate graph (qv) in which vertical scale is arranged in logarithmic cycles rather than straight arithmetical progression
locus	path described by point moving according to given law, eg: point moving at constant distance from second fixed point traces locus which is circular
logical tree	simple form of 'algorithm' (qv) showing choices or decisions available in given circumstances; broken down into sequence of 'yes/no' steps
logogram	sign or character standing for word
logotype (abb: logo)	letters or words forming distinctive whole, often used for trade name or brand name; originally, result of fusing two or three type characters on single type body (not necessarily as 'ligature')
long descenders	variants of typeface which have longer 'descenders' (qv) than normal, eg:

10 PT.

When jobs have type sizes fixed quickly margins

10 (LONG DESC.) ON 12 PT.

When jobs have type sizes fixed quickly margins

long letters	those type characters which take up almost whole of body, eg:

Q f

long 's'	type character used in printed English until early nineteenth century:

inſtruction *enſemble*

look-through	appearance of paper when viewed against light; also called 'see-through' in US
loose-leaf	one which permits leaves to be removed at will; see also 'ring-binder', 'multi-ring binder', 'Wire-O binder', 'plastic comb/coil binder' and 'binding methods'

99

low key	photographic image in which, by lighting and/or processing, most of tones are very dark:

lower-case (abb: lc)	small letters in typeface (a, b, c, d) as distinct from upper case/caps and small caps
long cross	same as 'dagger' (qv)
lpm	initials of 'lines per minute', rate at which 'computer output device' (qv) will print out typed lines; slowest printers operate at about 20 lpm, fastest at about 4,000 lpm
Ludlow	type composing machine involving hand assembly of matrices and machine casting in 'slug' (qv) form; used for newspaper headlines

M

machine composition	any operation producing type matter by means of keyboards and composing machines
machine direction	direction of sheet or web of paper corresponding to direction of travel in paper-making machine, from which comes 'grain' of fibres
machine-finished paper	uncoated paper smoothed on both sides, but not as glossy as super-calendered paper
machine-glazed paper	uncoated paper polished to high gloss on one side but left rough on other; suitable for posters

machine minder	skilled printing operative who sets up printing press and tends it during print run; known in US as 'pressman'
machine proof	first copies off printing machine before it begins full run, used as final check proof
machine readable	of data in general, those which can be read into computer by punched tape, magnetic disc, etc; of alphanumeric sets, those which can be read by 'OCR' and 'MICR' encoding equipment (qv)
machine sheet	any printed sheet off printing press during run
macron	horizontal line over vowel indicating that it is 'long', thus: tēdius.
macrophotography	photography of small objects by means of standard camera fitted with bellows extension or special lens extension tubes
magenta	red-blue colour containing no green; one of three primaries used in 'subtractive colour mixing' (qv)
magnetic ink characters	see 'MICR'
magnetic track (of cinefilm)	alternative to 'optical track' (qv), using stripe of recording medium; increasingly used for projection systems, it will eventually replace optical sound track
majuscules	upper-case characters, written or typeset
make-ready	preparing printing surface on press, ready for printing
make-up	to arrange type matter, blocks and spacing material into pages
making	one complete batch of paper from mill; large printing companies often buy whole making for themselves
manuscript (abb: MS, pl: MSS)	any written matter intended for typesetting (also called 'copy'); more specifically, handwritten, as against typewritten copy
manifold	very thin 'bank' paper (qv), used when large number of carbon copies is required
manilla	strong, buff-coloured paper used for envelopes and folders, made from fibrous hemp

map projections (global)	see 'cylindrical projections', 'Mollweide's equal-area projection', 'Sanson-Flamsteed's equal-area projection' and 'zenithal projections'
marbling	staining paper to produce effect of marble grain; used mainly for endpapers, especially of account books
marching display	in photocomposition, narrow display unit attached to keyboard which shows about 30–40 last characters keyed
margin-notched card	same as 'edge-notched card' (qv)
mark-up	see 'type mark-up'
married print	in cinefilm, finished print which has sound combined with picture on same film; also known as 'composite print'
masking	adjusting light values in photomechanical processing, especially of colour; also used as synonym for 'scaling' (qv) and 'cropping'
master proof	galley proof or page proof containing printer's corrections and queries, to which author's corrections are added and which is returned to printer
masthead	information about publishing house which appears above editorial of newspaper or on contents page of periodical; sometimes (inaccurately) used as synonym for 'nameplate' (qv)
mathematical signs	some type characters used in mathematical settings are:

$+$ plus
$-$ minus
$\div$ divided by*
$\times$ multiplied by**
$=$ equal to
$\neq$ not equal to
$\equiv$ identical with
$\not\equiv$ not identical with
$\approx$ approximately equal to

*   following are also valid:
$^{234}/_{123}$ or 234/123
**   in algebra, following are also valid:
xy or $x{\cdot}y$ (ie: x multiplied by y)

≃	proportional to
∞	varies directly as
>	less than
<	greater than
≥	equal to or less than
≤	equal to or greater than
∴	therefore
∵	because *or* since
√	square root
∛	cube root
‖	parallel to
⊥	perpendicular to
→	approaches
↔	mutually implies
∞	infinity
Σ	sum of
Π	product of
∫	integral sign

matrice alternative spelling of 'matrix' (qv)

matrix (general) womb: place where something is developed, formed

matrix, mat (character generation) mould for casting type character in machine composition; also, 'image-carrier' (qv) to photocomposition machine

matrix printer computer output device producing characters composed from 'dot matrix' (qv); also called 'needle printer'

matte in cinefilm and TV, mask used to blank off one part of negative during exposure to allow superimposition of another shot; 'travelling matte' involves shooting subject against plain blue background onto which is later imposed additional background scene (in TV this can be done simultaneously by electronic wizardry; often known as 'chroma-key')

mean-line upper limit of 'x-height' (qv): imaginary line running along tops of lower-case characters which do not have 'ascenders'; also known as 'x-line', especially in US

measure width to which any line of type is set, usually expressed in 12pt (pica) ems; distinction may be made between maximum line length (measure) and other, lesser, line lengths within this measure

mechanical	same as 'camera-ready art(work)'; term commonly used in US, much less so in UK
mechanical binding	one in which leaves are fastened by inserting metal or plastic units into holes punched or drilled through them; may be permanent, as in spiral binding, or loose-leaf, as in ring binder (see 'binding methods')
mechanical pulp	basis of newsprint and other cheap printing papers being untreated chemically; known in US as 'groundwood'
mechanical tints	patterns of dots or lines which are laid down on prescribed areas of artwork; may be applied either before or during processing proper
medium (pl: media)	in communications industry, means whereby information is conveyed: book, movie, newspaper, radio, TV; last three are often grouped as 'mass media'
Mercator's projection	see 'cylindrical projections (global)'
merge (of tape)	in photocomposition, to make corrections by preparing coded tape which is then combined with original uncorrected tape to produce third, fully corrected tape
metal halide lamp	photographic light source with rating up to 5,000 watts, consisting of very small discharge seal encased in outer bulb; also known as 'compact-source iodide lamp'

metric prefixes   these are:

micro-	= millionth	deca-	= ten times
milli-	= thousandth	hecto-	= hundred times
centi-	= hundredth	kilo-	= thousand times
deci-	= tenth	mega-	= million times

mf	initials of 'more follows'; inserted at foot of each page of newspaper copy except last one
MF (paper)	abbreviation for 'machine-finished' (qv)
MG (paper)	abbreviation for 'machine-glazed' (qv)
MICR	initials of 'magnetic ink character recognition'; use of special ink for machine reading of numerals and letters, especially for cheques and other banking applications, requiring special type designs:

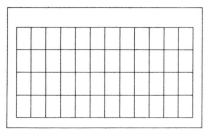

E13B

CMC7

microfiche | microform recording medium in which many images are arranged in rows on sheet of film and space is left for eye-legible title; there are various formats but those recommended by ISO are:

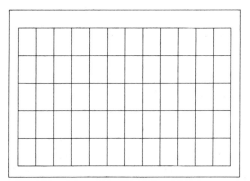

75 × 125mm format giving 48 images

105 × 148mm format giving 60 images

microfilm | used in data processing and for documentation and record compilation; material is most often filmed onto 16mm ('cine' or 'comic' formats) for use as reels:

16mm 'cine' format   *16mm 'comic' format*

105

microform	generic term for all kinds of microrecording, whether opaque or transparent
micro-opaque	microform record on opaque material, usually paper or card
middle (mid) space	one of three standard word spaces in handsetting, ¼em of set; other two are 'thin' and 'thick' (see 'word spacing')
military projection	see 'oblique projections'
mill ream	472 sheets of handmade or mould-made paper
millboard	hard, tough well rolled board with good finish; used for covers of account books and some case-bound printed books
mimeography	popular name for stencil ink-duplicating process, derived from trade name Mimeograph
miniature camera	see 'camera types'
minus leading	in photocomposition, reduction of space between lines of type to give line interval less than stated point size of type; unsuitable term, since 'lead' is not involved, ('negative linespacing' is preferred)
minus linespacing	same as 'minus leading' but not much better, as it is too cryptic
minuscules	lower-case characters, written or typeset
mix	same as 'dissolve' (qv)
MM Paper System	in US, attempt to standardize 'basis weight' (qv) by relating substance to 1,000 sheets of 1,000 square inch area
mock-up	rough simulation of newspaper, periodical or book, showing intended position of type matter and illustrations
modern face	class of typeface dating from late 18th century, characterized by fine hairlines and unbracketed serifs:

ABCabcdefg

| moiré pattern | fancy way of describing 'screen clash' (qv) but can best be applied to desirable use of this effect: |

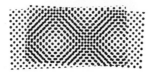

| Mollweide's equal-area projection | global projection in form of ellipse in which equator is twice length of central meridian; projection is much improved by interrupting it through oceans: |

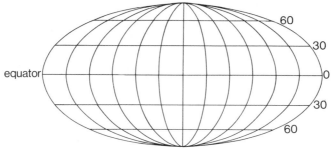

Mollweide's equal area

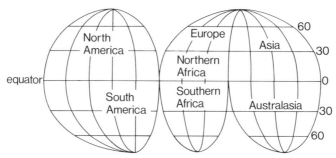

Mollweide's interrupted

| monograph | publication dealing with single object or person |

| monoline (typeface) | one in which all letter strokes are equal thickness (or seem to be); may be either sans-serif or slab-serif: |

ABCDefghIJKLmno

Monophoto	trade name for Monotype's photocomposition system
monorail camera	see 'camera types'
Monotype	two machines (keyboard and caster) which produce metal type in single characters, as distinct from Intertype and Linotype
montage	juxtaposition of two or more images so as to derive new meaning not present before; may be effected in space, as on a page, or in time, as in cinefilm (see also 'photomontage')
Morse code	alphabet invented by Samuel Morse in 1832 for transmitting telegraphic messages, using dots and dashes or long and short signals; since code is devised so that most commonly used vowels and consonants are represented by simplest grouping of dots and dashes, it makes most economical use of time and transmission power:

A	·—	N	—·	1	·————
B	—···	O	———	2	··———
C	—·—·	P	·——·	3	···——
D	—··	Q	——·—	4	····—
E	·	R	·—·	5	·····
F	··—·	S	···	6	—····
G	——·	T	—	7	——···
H	····	U	··—	8	———··
I	··	V	···—	9	————·
J	·———	W	·——	0	—————
K	—·—	X	—··—		
L	·—··	Y	—·——		
M	——	Z	——··		

mortised type	one which has part of body cut away to enable letter to fit closer; more common in larger sizes of ornamented wood types
mount	wood, metal or plastic base on which printing plate is fixed to bring it to type-height (qv) for letterpress printing
moving peg-bar	in film animation, 'peg-bar' (qv) equipped with geared movement to

108

achieve panning across field area of rostrum camera

Moviola — in cinefilm, trade name for popular make of 'editing machine' (qv)

MS (pl: MSS) — abbreviation for 'manuscript' (qv)

mull — in book production, net fabric fixed to back of book to assist in holding case to book

Müller-Lyer figures — pair of figures devised to demonstrate optical illusion; upper horizontal appears longer than lower one but in fact both are same length:

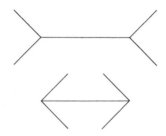

multiple exposure — in photography, exposing same image or different images on same film frame or same photoprint:

multi-ring binder — ring binder with more elaborate mechanism (see 'binding methods')

multiview
(multiplane)
projections

'orthographic projections' (qv) consisting of set of matched views of object, assembled as one drawing; views are best thought of as projected onto faces of glass box placed round object: two conventions exist: first angle projection (used in Europe and for building construction in UK) and third angle projection (used in US, Canada and for some engineering purposes in UK):

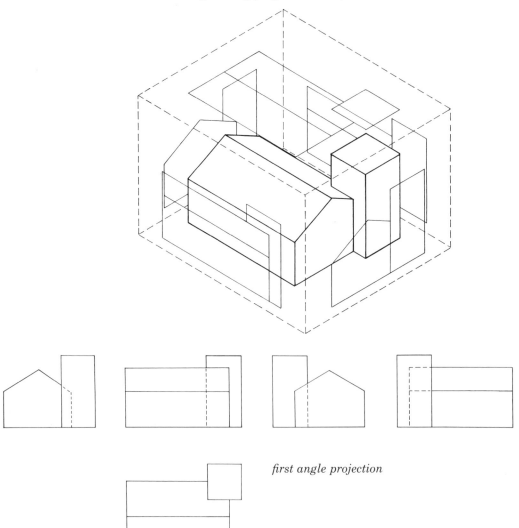

first angle projection

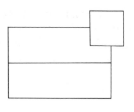

third angle projection

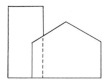 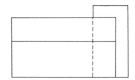 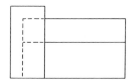

Munsell colour system — method of measuring colour which defines each colour according to three properties: 'hue', 'chroma' and 'value' (qqv)

mute roll/neg/print — in cinefilm, one lacking sound track

mutton, mutt — familiar name of 'em-quad' (qv)

nameplate (of newspaper) — title of newspaper in distinctive style, usually at top of page one, also known as 'flag'; sometimes incorrectly called 'masthead' (qv)

Necker's cube — one of several drawn figures used by perceptual psychologists to demonstrate visual ambiguity, pointed out by L. A. Necker in 1832; cube may be thought of as viewed either from above or below:

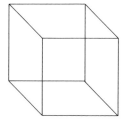

needle file	one using 'edge-notched cards' (qv)
needle printer	same as 'matrix printer' (qv)
negative line-feed	see 'reverse line-feed'
negative linespacing	in photocomposition, reduction of space between lines of type to give line interval less than stated point size of type; marginally preferred to 'minus leading' or 'minus linespacing' but still not recommended
network diagram	one which describes nature of connexions between elements by means of 'nodes' ('vertices') and 'branches' ('arcs')
newsprint	cheap, absorbent, unsized paper used for newspapers
next reading matter, next text matter	instruction form advertizer in periodical, requiring that advertisement be positioned next to part of editorial content
nick (of type)	groove in shank of type (qv)
nomogram, nomograph	arranging three scales so that straight-edge joining known values on two scales is extended to third scale to provide desired value
non-counting keyboard	in photocomposition, input device which gives operator no information on which to base 'end-of-line decisions' (qv)
non-lining figures	same as 'old-style figures' (qv)
nonpareil (pron: nomprl)	name of old type size which approximated to 6pt; now used to describe 6pt lead
np	initials of 'new paragraph', used in proof correction
nut	familiar name for 'en-quad' (qv)

oblique projections	parallel projections (qv) in which one face or object is parallel to plane of projection (picture plane) whilst visual rays (projectors) are inclined to plane of projection, as distinct from 'orthographic

projections'; there are three common types:

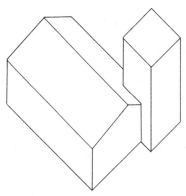

military (planometric): ground plane (plan) drawn parallel to plane of projection, vertical edges extended along inclined axis (usually, but not necessarily, 45°) at same scale or reduced scale

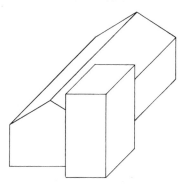

cavalier: front vertical plane (elevation) drawn parallel to plane of projection, receding edges extended along inclined axis at same scale

cabinet: as 'cavalier' but with receding edges drawn half-scale so as to give impression of fore-shortening

113

oblique roman	same as 'sloped roman' (qv); term more common in US
oblique stroke	see 'solidus'
OBR	initials of 'optical bar (code) recognition' (see 'bar code')
OCR	initials of 'optical character recognition': using electronic scanner to read copy set on special typewriter, thus eliminating one stage of input; character set used must be acceptable to scanner:

ABCDEFG 123456789

octavo, 8vo	cut or folded sheet which is one-eighth of basic sheet size
offcut	paper cut to waste when sheet is trimmed to size; may sometimes be used for another print job
off-line	any operation in computer-controlled work not directly connected with computer, and any output therefrom, as distinct from 'on-line'
offprint	feature or other portion of publication made available separately from whole work, especially for use of author; may be either 'run-on' of main printing or subsequent reprint (also known as 'separate')
offset photolithography, offset-litho, offset	usual commercial form of photolithography, in which inked image is first transferred to rubber blanket, then to paper:

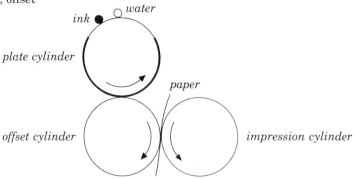

ogee	double curve which starts concave and becomes convex

OK subject to correction	instruction on proof giving qualified go-ahead for printer to print, provided required proof correction has been made
old-face (US: old-style)	class of typefaces dating from early 16th century:

ABC have work jobs

old-style figures	set of type numerals which includes some descenders, as distinct from 'lining figures' (qv): 1234567890
on-line	any operation in computer-controlled work which is directly connected to computer and any output matter resulting therefrom
one-point perspective	see 'perspective projections'
one-third reduction	amount to which 'half-up' (qv) artwork is reduced in processing
onion skin	highly glazed, very thin, translucent paper
op cit	abbreviation for *opere citato*, Latin for 'in the work quoted'; used in footnotes
opacity	degree to which (a) ink will obscure colour of material on which it is printed, or (b) paper will prevent 'see-through' (qv) or 'show-through' (qv)
opaquing	blocking out portion of film negative to prevent reproduction of processing fault or unwanted part of image
opaline	fine, translucent paper with high glaze, used for greeting cards
optical (as noun)	in cinefilm and TV, any special effect such as wipe, freeze frame, dissolve and fade
optical alignment	arranging certain characters, such as T, to project into left-hand margin so as to give better appearance:

DON'T TURN BACK

optical character recognition	see 'OCR'
optical coincidence card	same as 'peek-a-boo card' (qv) and 'optical stencil card'
optical printer	form of teletypewriter using cathode ray tube to project type character or line on sensitized surface to which black powder adheres; this is then transferred to paper
optical spacing	in typesetting, arranging letterspacing within line of caps to give more even effect; more correctly, 'optically even spacing'
optical stencil card	same as 'peek-a-boo card' (qv)
optical track	in cinefilm, normal method of incorporating sound on film by means of clear track of varying width running alongside image; see also 'magnetic track'
optical type fount	one intended for 'OCR' (qv)
Oracle	trade name for Independent Broadcasting Authority's system for transmitting 'teletext' (qv) news and information
ordinal numbers	first, second, third as distinct from cardinal numbers, one, two, three
ordinate	coordinate parallel to y-axis in 'coordinate graph' (qv)
original (print)	copy, whether specially prepared or not, which is to be reproduced
origination costs	those arising from 'print origination' (qv)
orihon	see 'zig-zag book'
ornament	see 'printer's ornament'
orthochromatic	applied to photographic film sensitive only to yellow, green and blue
orthographic projections	term used to cover those 'parallel projections' (qv) in which visual rays are perpendicular to plane of projection (picture plane), as distinct from 'oblique projections' (qv)
Ostwald system	method of measuring colour involving use of colour patch charts showing gradations of same 'hue' (qv) from pure through

	progressive shading to black and progressive tinting to white
out see copy	proof instruction directing printer to insert portion of copy which has been omitted
outboard computer	slang for one which is incorporated in device not connected on-line to large central computer and is confined to specific function
outer forme	one which includes outermost pages of folded section
outline letter	one in which inner part has been removed, thus:

ABCDEFGHIJK

outset	less common name for 'wrap-round' section (qv)
outwork	printing operations which cannot be done by main printer and are sub-contracted out
overhang cover	one which extends beyond trimmed leaves of book; may be either 'cased' or 'yapp' (qv)
overhead projector	one which uses large transparent cels or rolls, either prepared or drawn direct, and an overhead lens that turns projected image through 90 degrees
overlay	translucent or transparent material laid over piece of artwork or other original copy, on which instructions may be shown; also, one of series of separations in artwork drawn for colour reproduction
over-matter, overset	typeset matter which cannot be accommodated within space allocated in newspaper, periodical or book
overprint	printed addition to job already printed
overs, overruns	any part of print run in excess of quantity ordered, usually by intention, to allow for 'spoils' (qv)
ozalid	trade name of diazo process used for photocopy proofs of direct impression or photocomposition settings, and of made-up pages

P

page   one side of leaf of book, subdivided thus:

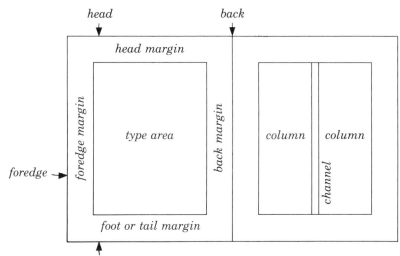

left hand page (lhp) or verso   right hand page (rhp) or recto

page make-up terminal	in photocomposition, display device which gives view of keyboarded copy made up as whole page; some terminals offer facsimile of composed matter, others an approximation
page printer	computer output device (qv) printing whole page at a time by means of xerography or electron beam recording
page(d) proof	proof from from print matter after it has been made up into pages
Page View Terminal (PVT)	trade name for one make of 'page make-up terminal' (qv)
pages-to-view	number of pages appearing on one side of sheet; thus 16 page section would normally be '8 pages-to-view' (see also 'imposition')
paginate	to number pages of book consecutively (see also 'foliation')
pan-and-tilt head	mounting attachment permitting camera (still or movie) to be

rotated or tilted smoothly

panning   in cinefilm and TV, rotating camera on mount during shooting, thus:

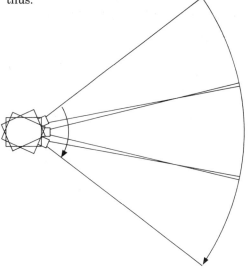

panoramic camera   one with scanning lens which throws very wide image onto curved plate or film

pantograph   device consisting of articulated rods, pointer and pen, used to copy any image to reduced or enlarged scale:

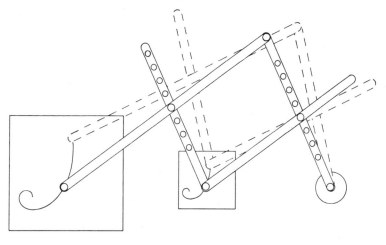

Pantone system	trade name for colour-matching system covering inks, papers, pens and gouache	

paper sizes and sub-divisions, except 'A, B and C series of paper sizes' (qv)

traditional UK paper sizes derived from wide variety of independent needs and were not related rationally; most commonly used for printing were:

foolscap	$13\frac{1}{2} \times 17$in	these are 'broadsheet' sizes; double
crown	15×20in	and quad sizes are arrived at by
large post	$16\frac{1}{2} \times 21$in	doubling and quadrupling folio, 4to
demy	$17\frac{1}{2} \times 22\frac{1}{2}$in	and 8vo sizes by halving, quartering
medium	18×23in	and dividing by eight
royal	20×25in	

since 1970, UK printers, publishers and paper makers have agreed on following rationalization of untrimmed sheet sizes:

metric quad crown	768×1008mm
metric quad large crown	816×1056mm
metric quad demy	888×1128mm
metric quad royal	960×1272mm
RA0	860×1220mm
SRA0	900×1280mm

with these subdivisions for trimmed book sizes:

	quarto	octavo
metric crown	264×189mm	186×123mm
metric large crown	258×201mm	198×129mm
metric demy	276×219mm	216×138mm
metric royal	312×237mm	234×156mm
A4 297×210mm		
A5 210×148mm		

In US there is at time of writing no official rationalization of paper but moves are afoot to promote changeover to metric standards; most commonly used sheet sizes are 25×38in, 26×40in and 36×48in; common sizes for trimmed stationery are $11 \times 8\frac{1}{2}$in and $10 \times 7\frac{1}{2}$in

paperback	book with paper cover, also known as 'softback' or 'soft cover' and in US (if of small format) as 'pocketbook'
paper-to-paper	see 'fold-to-paper'
papyrus	writing material made from pressed stalks of large reed; used in ancient Egypt, Greece and Rome

120

University of Cumbria

Learning, Information and
Student Services
Tel. 01228 616 218

Borrowed Items 14/11/2011 13:42:20
XXX3363

Item Title	Due Date
* Illustrated graphics glossary : of	21/11/2011
Print and production finishes for t	24/11/2011
Invasion Prague 68	24/11/2011
War posters : weapons of mass c	24/11/2011
Soviet posters : the Sergo Grigor	24/11/2011
Making handmade books : 100+	24/11/2011
Help! : soziale appelle = Help : so	24/11/2011
Political posters in Central and E:	30/11/2011
Packaging prototypes	07/12/2011
Experimental formats & packagin	07/12/2011
1000 package designs : a comple	07/12/2011
Paper : tear, fold, rip, crease, cut	07/12/2011

* Indicates items borrowed today

E: lissfusehill@cumbria.ac.uk
Website: www.cumbria.ac.uk/liss

parabola	'locus' (qv) of point which moves so that its distances from fixed point and from fixed straight line are always equal; see also 'conic sections'
paragraph mark	type character indicating beginning of new paragraph, usually as alternative to indention; also used as sixth order of 'reference marks' (qv)
parallax error	in photography, difference between what is seen through viewfinder and what is recorded on film, especially evident in twin-lens reflex camera:

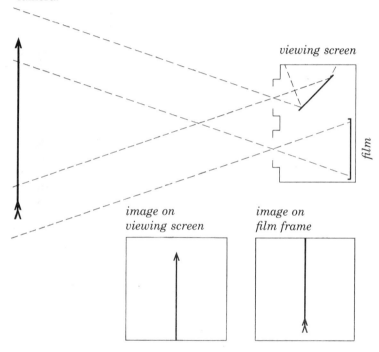

parallel	type character used as fifth order of 'reference marks' (qv) for footnotes
parallel fold	folding sheet once, then again along line parallel to first fold (see 'folding methods')
parallel projections	drawing projections in which observer is considered to be at infinity, so that 'visual rays' (also called 'projectors') are parallel to

each other; see also 'perspective projections', 'oblique projections' and 'orthographic projections':

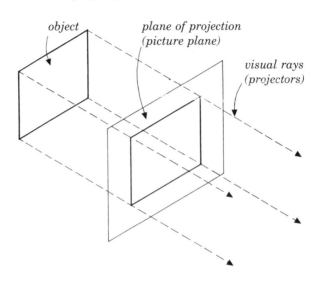

parameter	variable quantity given fixed value for specific calculation; often misused as synonym for 'limit'
parentheses	see 'brackets'
pars pro toto	Latin for 'the part standing for the whole'; common device in graphic communication (also known as 'synecdoche')
pass	one cycle of operation through printing or photocomposition machine; may involve more than one impression or transfer of image
passim	Latin for 'here-and-there'; used in footnotes
paste-up	any copy prepared for reproduction which comprises several elements assembled and pasted up as one; in addition, may refer to layout assembly used as guide to printer, not for reproduction
pasting in/on	same as 'tipping in/on' (qv)
patent	licence guaranteeing exclusive rights to inventor of 'any manner of new manufacture and any new method or process of testing

applicable to the improvement or control of manufacture'

PCMI   initials of 'photo-chromic micro-imaging', relatively new 'microform' process capable of reduction ratios up to 200×

PE   initials of 'printer's error', indication on proof that error is made by typesetter and does not originate from author; US convention not common in UK (see also 'AA')

peculiar   same as 'special sort' (qv)

peek-a-boo card index   one composed of 'feature cards', each of which contains an identical array of code numbers but which have varying patterns of holes punched to denote particular features, or 'descriptors', of subject:

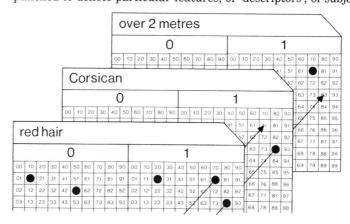

peg-bar   in film animation, device for holding film cels in register by means of shaped holes in cels which fit over 'pegs' or 'pins' in thin metal strip (see 'rostrum')

pel   see 'picture element'

pentagram   five-pointed star formed by extending sides of pentagon, thus:

pentaprism	in photography, five-sided prism which converts image on ground glass screen of reflex camera to right way round and right way up:
perfect binding	binding method (qv) in which cut backs of leaves of book are secured by synthetic glue; also known as 'threadless binding' or 'unsewn binding'
perfecting	printing second, or reverse, side of sheet; also called 'backing up'
perfecting press, perfector	'rotary press' (qv) which prints both sides of paper in one pass through machine (though not simultaneously)
perforating at press	using sharpened, slotted rule locked into forme to produce dot or dash perforation in sheet
period	common US term for 'full point'
peripheral (as noun)	any device connected to computer which is not part of its central processor unit (CPU)
perspective projections	drawing projections in which observer is considered to be stationed at finite point, as distinct from 'parallel projections' (qv):

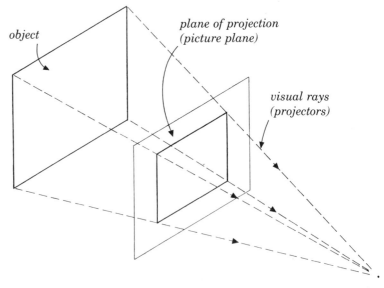

object

plane of projection
(picture plane)

visual rays
(projectors)

station
point

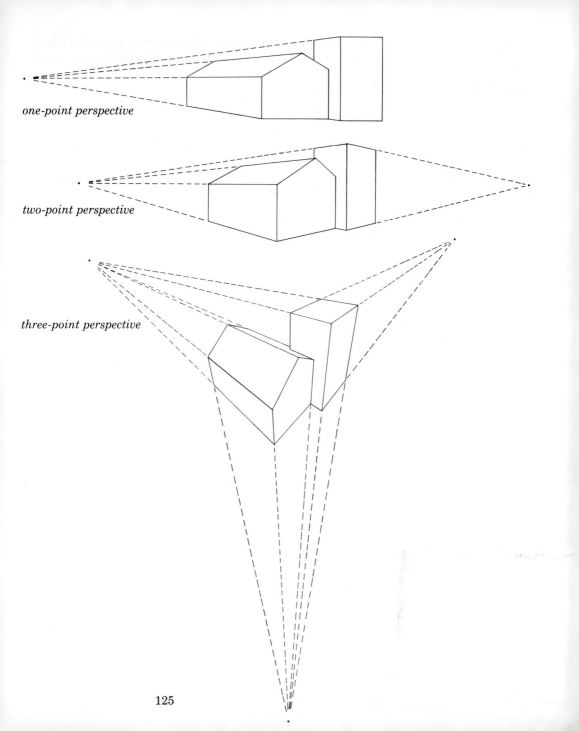

one-point perspective

two-point perspective

three-point perspective

125

PERT	initials of 'Programme Evaluation and Review Technique': method of network analysis with close similarities to 'CPA/CPM', (qv) with which it is now practically synonymous
phonogram	written symbol representing spoken sound
phosphor	fluorescent substance used to coat inside of cathode ray tubes and fluorescent lamps
photocomposition	preferred term for any system of typesetting by photographic means, also known as 'phototypesetting' and inaccurately as 'photosetting' (but see also 'filmsetting'); photocomposition machines have developed through four stages, or generations:

first generation
those designed in close imitation of hot-metal machines
second generation
those using electromechanical systems which control mirrors, escapements and lenses
third generation
those generating type characters by means of cathode ray tubes
fourth generation
those involving use of lasers for exposure of image onto film or paper

photocopy	photographic copy from original; 'photostat' is one kind of photocopy
photodirect lithography	process using plates made direct from original artwork without intermediate (negative) stage
photodisplay unit	same as 'photoheadliner'
photoengraving	photomechanical etching process which produces a letterpress line or halftone plate
photoflood lamp	photographic light source similar in shape and size to ordinary domestic lamp but about 2½ - 3 times brighter
photogelatin process	another name for 'collotype' (qv)
photogram	photographic image created without use of camera or film, by exposing photographic paper to light and throwing shadows on it
photogravure	photomechanical 'intaglio' (qv) printing process in which impression

is taken from pattern of recessed dots (cells) of varying depth:

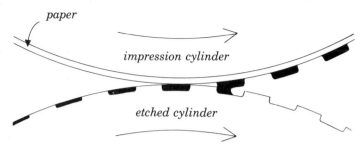

paper

impression cylinder

etched cylinder

photoheadliner	machine producing display type by photographic means: letter-spacing may be either automatic or manual, and many makes have special lenses for condensing, expanding, slanting and otherwise distorting letter forms
photolitho(graphy)	photomechanical version of 'lithography' (qv); see also 'offset'
photomechanical	complete assembly or type matter, line artwork and halftone artwork onto transparent base as film positive
photomechanical transfer (PMT)	process particularly suited to rapid production of line photoprints for paste-up artwork
photomontage	juxtaposition or superimposition of photographic images so that new meaning or impression is drawn from their combination, eg:

Photopake	trade name for opaque paint used for blocking out process negatives

photoprint	used in photocomposition to describe equivalent of repro proof in machine compositon
photosetting	vague term best avoided, but used to embrace all machines producing reproduction proofs of type images, whether for display or text matter, on film or paper
photostat, stat	trade name, now accepted as general, for thin photocopy used as part of paste-up layout or presentation visual
photostatic printing	see 'xerography'
phototelegraphy	see 'wire-photo'
phototypesetting	alternative term for 'photocomposition' (qv)
photounit	output component of photocomposition machine which does typesetting and production of phototype
pica (typewriter)	larger of the two commonest typewriter faces (qv)
pica, pica em	12pt em, standard unit of typographic measurement for type line length and spacing; 4.216mm (0.1660in); loosely known as 'em' in UK, so that when referring to space which is not in picas it is best to specify '– ems of set'
pica gauge/rule	same as 'type scale' (qv)
pi characters	US term for 'special sorts' or 'peculiars', now in use in UK due to importation of US photocomposition machines
picking	break up of small portions of paper surface during printing, caused by tackiness of ink; also known as 'pulling' or 'plucking'
pictogram, pictograph	pictorial sign; that is, one resembling the thing it stands for:

picture element	in CRT scanning or picture synthesis, one of large number of encoded observations of subject which comprise recorded picture; known also as 'pel' or 'pixel' (ugh)
picture plane	same as 'plane of projection' (qv)
pie (pi in US)	printer's term for metal type which has become mixed by accident
pie graph/chart'	one in which proportions of whole are represented as slice segments of circular pie; also known as 'divided circle' and 'wheel graph':

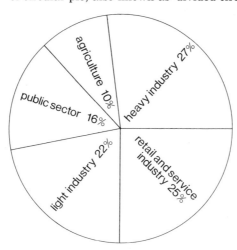

piece accent	see 'floating accent'
piece fraction	in typesetting, fraction made up from more than one piece of type; also known as 'split fraction'
pin matrix	same as 'dot matrix' (qv)
pixel	see 'picture element'
PL/1	see 'computer languages'
plane of projection (abb:PP)	in 'parallel projections' and 'perspective projections' (qv), imaginary plane (usually vertical) interposed between object and 'station point', onto which image of object is projected; also known as 'picture plane'

planning table	same as 'lining-up table' (qv)
planographic	said of printing process such as lithography, in which printing surface is neither raised (relief) nor incised (intaglio)
planometric projection	see 'oblique projections'
plastic comb/coil binding	see 'binding methods'
plate (printing)	metal, rubber or plastic surface from which impression is taken
plate (in book)	illustration on different paper from that used for text
plate camera	see 'camera types'
plate cylinder	in 'offset photolithography' (qv), one which carries inked plate, as against 'blanket cylinder'
platen press	letterpress machine in which paper is pressed onto type matter from flat surface called a platen; one which has flat impression as distinct from cylindrical one:

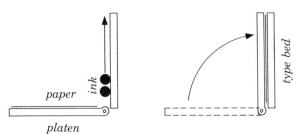

plucking	same as 'picking' (qv)
PMS	initials of 'Pantone Matching System'; prefix attached to colour samples and specifications which employ that system
PMT (photoprint)	trade mark made from abbreviation for 'photomechanical transfer' (qv)
pocketbook	'paperback book' (qv) small enough to fit into pocket (term more common in US)

130

pocket envelope	one with opening and flap on shorter side, as distinct from 'banker envelope':

point (Anglo-American)	basic unit of typographic measurement: 0.351mm (0.013837in); 12 pts = 1 pica em
point (Didot)	equivalent to Anglo-American point, used in most European countries: 0.375mm (0.0148in); 12 Didot points = one cicero or *corps douze*
polarizing filter	in photography, one used mainly to get rid of unwanted reflexions from water, glass and polished surfaces; may also be used to darken blue skies in colour photography
Polaroid	trade name for self-developing photographic materials and special equipment they require; process was invented in 1947 by Edwin Land and is variant of 'DTR' process (qv)
Polaroid back	special holder fitted to conventional camera to hold Polaroid film
polygon	see 'regular polygon'
POP	initials of 'Post Office Preferred'; range of envelope and postcard sizes recommended by UK Post Office, which include ISO envelope sizes DL and C6 (see 'A, B and C series of paper sizes)
pop-on	in film animation, instantaneous appearance of new image in existing scene
population pyramid	see 'pyramid graph'
portrait format	describes proportion of film, photoprint, artwork or any piece of print matter in which height is appreciably longer than width
pos, pozzy	slang for 'positive transparency', with particular reference to those used in platemaking process

post binder	see 'binding methods'
post sync	in cinefilm, recording sound to match image after shooting
postal trap	any mailed piece (eg: unsealed envelope) which may trap another during collection, sorting or delivery
posterization	separating range of tones in continuous-tone original into flat, graded tones, using several negatives, one for each grade, then making composite print of them all; also called 'tone separation'
postlims	see 'end-matter'
pothooks	curved terminals of some type characters, especially in italics
p, pp	abbreviation for 'page', 'pages'
PP	abbreviation for 'picture plane' (qv)
pragmatics	see 'semiotic(s)'
preferred position	in periodical and newspaper publishing, an advantageous position for advertisements, such as one facing important editorial page; usually costs more
prelims	short for 'preliminary pages', those pages of book preceding main body (see also 'end matter'); following sequence is offered as reasonable but not immutable:

half- (or bastard) title *recto*
list of other works by same author or in same series *verso*
frontispiece *verso* (could face any *recto* in prelims)
title *recto*
bibliographical note and imprint *verso*
dedication and/or quotation (epigraph) *recto*
preface/foreword *recto or verso* (or after contents)
acknowledgements *recto or verso* (or in end-matter)
list of contents *recto*
list of illustrations *recto or verso*
introduction *recto or verso* (may be considered as part of main text)

pre-make-ready	in printing, all those operations carried out on formes or printing plates to reduce time spent making ready on machine, eg: register checks, 'interlays' (qv)

preprint	part of publication printed before main production, usually as loose sheet intended to be dropped into bound copies
presentation visual	careful representation which may be drawn, photoprinted, typeset or an amalgam of these, to show intended effect of printed job; known in US as 'comprehensive' or 'comp'
press proof	last proof to be read before giving an OK to print
pressure bar/slide	same as 'plastic grip/slide binder' (see 'binding methods')
pressure-sensitive	used to describe 'transfer lettering' (qv)
Prestel	trade name of UK Post Office's 'Viewdata' (qv) service
primary colours	those from which all other colours may be mixed, ie: red, blue, green for 'additive colour' (qv) and red-blue (magenta), blue-green (cyan), yellow for 'subtractive colour mixing' (qv) it is best to refer to these as 'additive primary colours' and 'subtractive primary colours', to avoid confusion
print origination	preparatory work of print job up to proofing stage
print-out	computer output via teleprinter, line printer or graph plotter; print-out may be either alphanumeric or graphic
print run	action of printing prescribed quantity of copies; quantity itself
print to paper	instruction to printer to use all available supply of paper rather than precisely specified number of copies
printability	degree to which an original, material or other intended component will contribute to an effective piece of print
printer's flower	type ornament in form of small flower or plant:

printer's ornament	generic term covering all type matter intended to create decorative effects, such as borders, arabesques and flowers
printer's reader	one who corrects proofs at printer's before they are sent to author

printer's terms and conditions	cunning network of escape clauses, set in 3pt type and printed in invisible ink on reverse of printer's estimate
printing-down frame	same as 'vacuum printing frame' (qv)
printing processes	fall into five main classes: those in which impression is taken from raised portions of surface (relief printing), those in which impression is taken from recesses in surface (intaglio printing), those in which impression is taken from flat surface treated chemically (planographic printing), those in which impression is made through stencil, and those in which no impression is involved

examples of these classes are:

relief	*intaglio*
woodcut	metal engraving
linocut	etching
letterpress	gravure

planographic	*stencil*
lithography	screen
collotype (photogelatin)	ink duplicating (mimeograph)
hectography (gelatin duplicating)	

no impression:
photostatic (xerography)*
ink-jet
*this process involves contact but not pressure

printmaking	any fine-art reproduction process, usually etching, woodcut, wood or steel engraving, or silkscreen
pro-forma	invoice or statement rendered before supply of goods or services, usually to meet budget deadline
process camera	one constructed especially for photomechanical reproduction processes; also called 'graphic arts camera'
process engraving	making letterpress printing plate by printing down photographic image onto plate and etching to form relief printing surface
process inks	those used in 'four-colour' and 'three-colour process' (qv)
process white	gouache specially made for use in artwork for reproduction
program	set of instructions devised to tell computer how to execute task

progressives (abb: progs)	series of proofs showing each plate of colour set in sequence, individually and in registered combination
proof	any preliminary impression from composed type matter or plates, for purpose of checking or revising before printing; but see also 'repro proof'
proof reader	any person who reads proofs for purpose of checking or revising before printing
proof reader's marks	agreed set of signs used by editors, proof readers and others concerned with copy preparation and proof correction
proofing press	one used for making proofs rather than making print run; usually small machine not made for fast, prolonged runs
proportional dividers	device for enlarging or reducing dimensions for drawings, or making conversions such as feet to metres
proportional scale	simple device for scaling photo and artwork (see 'scaling'):

proportional typewriter	one which spaces characters proportionally, so that 'i' occupies less width than 'w', for example; typewriters used for strike-on composition are almost without exception proportional
protractor	drawing instrument for measuring angles:

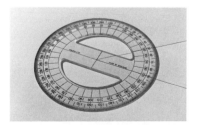

proud	type matter standing away from general body of matter on page is said to be 'proud' or 'standing proud'
prove	'to prove' is to make a proof
publisher's reader	one who reads and reports to publisher on submitted manuscripts
publisher's ream	one containing 516 sheets; also known as 'perfect ream'
puff	slang for favourable editorial comment in newspaper or periodical, usually tied in with paid advertisement
pull	same as 'proof' (qv)
pull-out	same as 'fold-out' (qv)
pull-out section	portion of periodical intended to be pulled out; not necessarily complete 'section' in technical sense (could be centre 4pp of 16pp section)
pulling	same as 'picking' (qv)
pulp	fibrous material of vegetable origin, from which paper is made; may be produced either by chemical or mechanical means, or combination of both
punching shapes	those available for various mechanical binding forms, both loose-leaf and permanent, are:

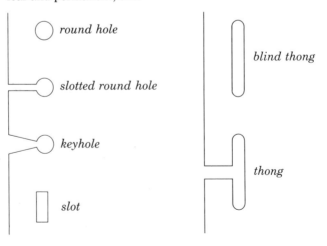

round hole

slotted round hole

keyhole

slot

blind thong

thong

put down/put up	instruction to printer: change to lower-case/change to caps
put to bed	when letterpress formes, lithoplates or gravure plates are secured to presses ready for printing, they are said to be 'put to bed'
PVT	initials of 'Page View Terminal' (qv)
pyramid graph	form of 'coordinate graph' (qv) devised mainly to display specific information about population:

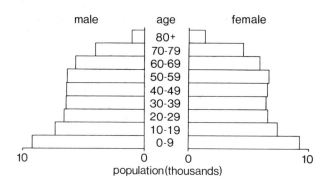

quad	type space, most commonly as 'em-quad' or 'en-quad' (qqv) but also available in widths of 1½, 2, 3 and 4 ems of set
quadding	driving abnormal space (eg: en-quads and em-quads) between words in order to fill out line; also used in reference to ranging left and right ('quad left/quad right') and centring ('quad centre') in linecaster composition and photocomposition
quadrilateral	plane figure bounded by four straight lines; there are six types:

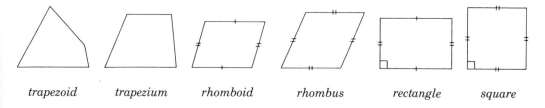

trapezoid   *trapezium*   *rhomboid*   *rhombus*   *rectangle*   *square*

quarto, 4to	cut or folded sheet which is one quarter of basic sheet size
quartz iodine lamp	see 'tungsten halogen lamp'
quire	one twentieth of 'ream' (qv); usually 24 or 25 sheets
quoin (pron: coyn)	in letterpress, expandable device used to take up space and lock up type 'forme' (qv) ready for press
quotes, quote marks	usually, inverted commas before, and apostrophes after, a word, phrase or passage of text to show that it is quoted (but note that typeface in this work uses commas reversed left-to-right, not inverted)
qv (pl: qqv)	abbreviation for *quod vide*, Latin for 'which see'; used in footnotes and glossaries to indicate cross reference
QWERT/QWERTY keyboard	standard typewriter keyboard layout, derived from order of characters on first alphabetic line (qwertyuiop); also commonly used for photocomposition keyboards

R

®	registered design mark, used to indicate that design has been officially registered, as measure of protection against plagiarism
RA paper sizes	see 'A, B and C Series'
radix	basis of any number system; in decimal system, radix is 10, and in binary system, radix is 2
rag paper	one largely made from rag pulp; used for best quality writings
ragged left/right	setting lines of type so that, though they are all set to standard measure, word spaces are not adjusted to make both edges align vertically (see 'ranged')
RAM	in computer usage, initials of 'random-access memory'; often used as working space in preprogrammed or 'ROM' (qv) programmed machine

Rand tablet	trade name for make of 'digitized pad' (qv)
raised capital	same as 'cocked-up initial' (qv)
raised point/dot	full point raised from usual position on base line (.) to position halfway up cap height (·) usually as decimal point, eg: 29·5; also known in US as 'centered dot'
ranged left/right	if one edge of block of type lines is said to be 'ragged' or 'unjustified', the other is 'ranged':

Existing on-line systems have made it possible to   *ragged right*
obtain bibliographic references in seconds – but have
only partly tackled the problem of obtaining the
original document, a process which can take weeks.

ragged left   Existing on-line systems have made it possible to
obtain bibliographic references in seconds – but have
only partly tackled the problem of obtaining the
original document, a process which can take weeks.

ranging figures	same as 'lining figures' (qv) but less suitable term
raster	screen, whether of halftone process or CRT scan (from German)
raw tape	same as 'unjustified tape' (qv) and 'idiot tape'
reaction shot	in cinefilm and TV, 'cutaway' (qv) to show reaction of one of film characters to main action
reader	see 'copyreader', 'printer's reader' and 'publisher's reader'
real time processing	in computer usage, processing in which machine's instructions keep time with process they are controlling, as in landing an aircraft
ream	standard quantity of paper containing 472, 480, 500, 504 or 516 sheets, according to nature of material; but note that in Europe, paper is now standardized in units of 1,000 (mille)
rear projection	same as 'back projection' (qv)
recto	any right-hand page of book; one which is odd-numbered

redundancy	in communication studies, way in which messages are reinforced by repetition and syntax to avoid misunderstanding by recipient:

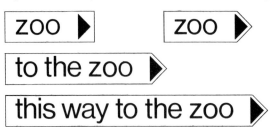

reel-fed	same as 'web-fed' (qv)
reference marks	those type characters which key footnotes to text above, usually appearing in following order:

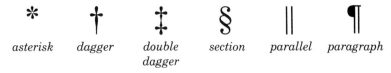

register	two or more print impressions in their correct relationship on sheet; hence 'in register' and 'out of register'
register marks	marks on a printed sheet appearing outside area of job when trimmed to size, used to ensure accurate register
registered design	one which has been accepted as such by Patent Office, 'design' in this case being defined as 'features of shape, configuration, pattern or ornament applied to an article by any industrial process or means'
regular polygon	plane figure having equal angles and equal sides; some regular polygons are:

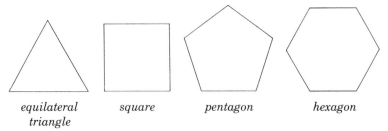

regular solid

one bounded by plane surfaces which are 'regular polygons' (qv); there are five regular convex solids:

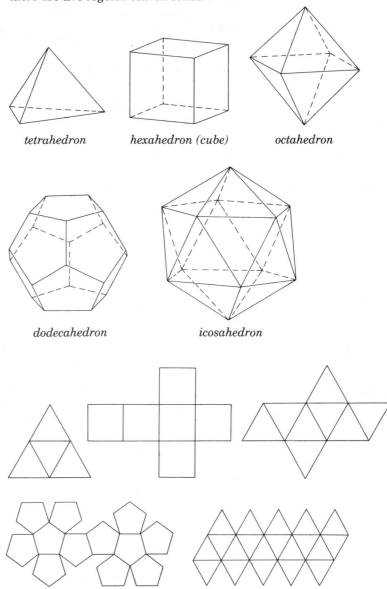

tetrahedron   *hexahedron (cube)*   *octahedron*

dodecahedron   *icosahedron*

opened-out patterns of regular solids

release print	in cinefilm, final print intended for showing to audience; also known as 'showprint'
relief printing	general term for those printing processes in which inked image is on raised surface, as in letterpress or flexography
relief stamping	same as 'die-stamping' (qv)
remainders	copies of book which is no longer selling at its original published price, reduced to clear stock; fate worse than death for any author
remote access	technique of accessing computer direct from distant terminal over communication lines
reprint	make subsequent printing (impression) of publication; reprints of single features or distinct portions of publication are known as 'separates' or 'offprints' (though these may also be part of first impression)
repro, repro proof	proof from type matter, made with great care on special proofing press using best quality coated paper, for use in photomechanical reproduction
reprographic printing	general term to cover work done by spirit duplicating, ink duplicating, electrostatic printing and small offset printing
reprotyping	typing intended for photomechanical reproduction
resin-coated paper	photographic material in which sensitized paper is sandwiched between polyethylene layers; also known as 'PE' or 'RC' paper
resolution	in photography and photomechanical reproduction ability of lens, film or mirror system to allow fine detail to be produced and read; sometimes expressed in terms of lines per centimetre
retainer fee	sum of money exacted annually by consultant designer from client for doing nothing in particular
reticulation	in photography, wrinkling and crazing of emulsion of film, causing grain to cluster in visible blobs
retouching	skilled alteration of halftone originals to improve or correct, using 'airbrush' (qv), brush, pencil, scalpel or dyes

retree	name for substandard batch of paper
reversal film	normal form of colour film, in which image is positive and can be projected as slide; also, special purpose contact film in which tone values of original are kept
reverse b to w	instruction to printer: reverse image from black to white
reverse field VDT	terminal which can display dark images on light background as alternative; also known as 'reverse contrast'
reverse indent	see 'hanging indent'
reverse l to r	instruction to printer: reverse image from left to right
reverse leading	see 'reverse line-feed'
reverse line-feed	in photocomposition, facility for turning film or paper back to previously set line so as to make additions, useful in tabular setting; also known as 'negative line-feed' (unsuitable because of ambiguity about 'negative') and 'reverse leading' (unsuitable because of reference to hot-metal setting)
reverse out	same as 'save out' (qv)
reverse out type	in photomechanical reproduction, instruction to 'save out' type image from background
reverse P	colloquialism for 'paragraph mark' (qv)
reverse-reading	reading right to left, as on letterpress printing surface or on some photocomposition film output; also known as 'wrong-reading'
revise (proof)	additional proof to show that corrections from earlier proof have been properly made
RF	in cartography, initials of 'representative fraction', used to denote scale relationship between distance shown on map and actual distance on ground, eg: 1/50,000
rhp	initials of 'right-hand page'
right-angle fold	folding a piece of paper in half, then in half again at right angle; standard fold for book sections (see 'folding methods')

right-reading	reading left to right, as on offset lithography printing plate
ring binder	see 'binding methods'
RIP	initials of 'rest in proportion'; instruction to indicate that all elements are to be reduced or enlarged in same proportion
rising front	device on some cameras whereby lens can be adjusted in relation to film so that 'converging verticals' (qv) can be corrected:

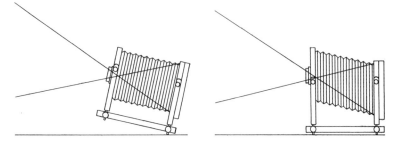

river	undesirable white streak straggling down through lines of type, caused by coinciding word spaces; sometimes known as 'window'
roller caption	in cinefilm and TV, titles and credits to movie or feature, set out on roll of black paper which is wound through aperture on machine and shot by camera:

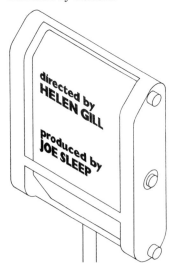

rolling ball (VDT)	attachment to VDT, which permits operator to change or adapt images on screen:

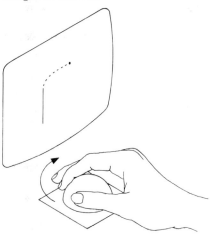

rom	abbreviation used in proof correction to show that word of passage should be reset in upright type
ROM	in computer usage, initials of 'read-only memory': part which holds predetermined instructions or program
roman	very general term to cover all typefaces deriving from humanistic manuscripts, as distinct from black letter (gothic); also used to distinguish non-italic letter forms
roman numerals	before introduction of arabic numerals, roman numbers were the norm, but are now only used for chapter headings, lists and dates; capital letters are used, in the following manner:

I	II	III	IV	V	VI	VII	VIII	IX	X
one	two	three	four	five	six	seven	eight	nine	ten
L	C		D		M				
fifty	one hundred		five hundred		one thousand				

ROP	1) initials of 'run-of-press'; instruction to printer to run off all paper available for particular job, regardless of job order 2) in newspapers, colour work printed with body of paper (run of paper), as against pre-printed colour
rose diagram	see 'star graph'

| rostrum (film animation) | camera mount with movable carriage for camera and movable tabletop for artwork beneath it; also known as 'animation stand': |

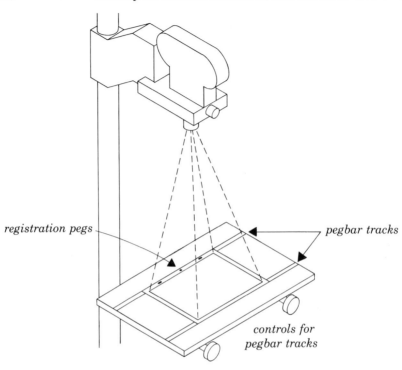

registration pegs — *pegbar tracks*

controls for pegbar tracks

rotary press   machine in which printing surface is cylindrical; may be either 'sheet-fed' or 'web-fed' (qv):

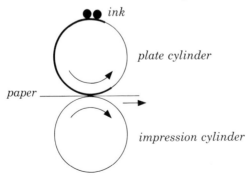

ink

plate cylinder

paper

impression cylinder

rotogravure   photogravure printing on web-fed rotary press

rough	sketch design for printed material, not always as 'rough' as term implies; there is even, ludicrous as it may seem, a 'finished rough'
round 'and'	same as 'ampersand' (qv)
rounding and backing	shaping book after sewing so that back is convex and foredge concave and to provide an edge on which to secure cover boards:

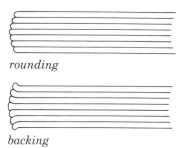

rounding

backing

Rubin's vase/face figure	image devised by E Rubin in 1915 and used by perceptual psychologists and others to demonstrate visual ambiguity arising from figure/ground confusion

rubric	heading of book chapter or section, printed in red to contrast with text in black
ruling-up table	same as 'lining-up table' (qv)
ruling pen	precision drawing instrument suitable for fine artwork:

run	see 'print run'
run-of-paper	in periodical and newspaper publishing, any placing of advertisement which is not especially advantageous (see also 'preferred position')
run on	1) proof correction or manuscript alteration: 'do not start new line or paragraph' (US: run in) 2) item often listed in print quotations, giving price for increasing print quantity by specified amount, eg: £100 per 1,000 'run on'
run-through work	use of special ruling machine to print parallel lines across sheet from one edge to other without breaks; see also 'feint lines'
runaround	typesetting in which lines of type are set to fit round an illustration or other display matter
runners	marginal numbers placed at regular intervals to give quick reference for text lines, especially of poetry
running head(line)	type lines above main text, giving book title and/or chapter title

S

saccadic movement	brief, rapid eye movement from one fixed point to another, as when reading
saddleback book	one having 'insetted work' which is secured through back fold by wire or thread stitches
saddle-stitch, saddle-wire	to secure book by means of thread or wire through back fold of insetted work; though 'saddle-stitch' is often used for wire as well as thread, this is not recommended because of possible confusion
safe area	in TV, that central portion of transmitted picture which can be guaranteed to remain visible on ordinary domestic receiver
safelight	in photography, coloured lamp used in darkrooms when developing or printing sensitized materials
same-size (abb: s/s)	instruction to printer to make print image same size as original

sans serif, sanserif	type face not having finishing strokes at ends of character elements:

ABC abc

Sanson-Flamsteed's equal-area projection	global projection in which equator is twice length of central meridian and poles are pointed, as distinct from 'Mollweide's projection' (qv); projection is much improved by interrupting it through oceans:

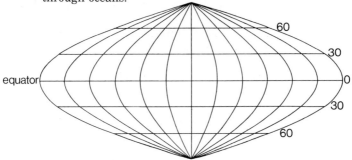

Sanson-Flamsteed's equal area

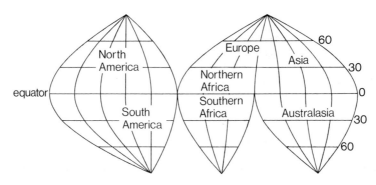

Sanson-Flamsteed's interrupted

SAP	see 'ASAP'
save out	in photomechanical reproduction, to produce white lettering or line image on solid or halftone ground
SC paper	abbreviation for 'supercalendered paper' (qv)

149

| scaling, scaling-up | working out degree of enlargement or reduction of original for reproduction, so that this can be shown by dimension and percentage marks on overlay; arrived at by means of 'diagonal' method or 'proportional scale' method: |

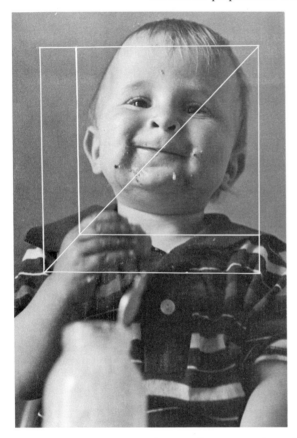

larger white rectangle in illustration on left is actual size required; this is contracted as diagonal to form smaller rectangle; final image is on right

| scamp | used in advertising to describe quick sketch not intended to show more than general idea |

| sc, s caps | abbreviations for 'small caps' (qv) |

| scanner | in photomechanical reproduction, photoelectronic device which |

'reads' relative densities of primary colours in full-colour copy to make colour separations

scatter graph   one representing separate values which may not be connected as line graph and which give only general trend of relationship:

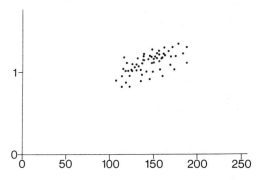

scatter proofs   in photomechanical processing, proofs of illustrations in random pattern unrelated to layout

Schuster's fork   impossible figure devised by Schuster in 1964; also known as 'Devil's tuning fork':

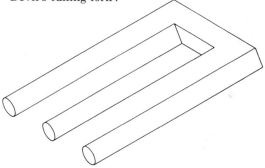

score   same as 'crease' (qv)

scraperboard   drawing material with heavy coating of china clay which can be scraped after covering with black ink to give an effect of 'white-line' engraving; also called 'scratchboard' (especially in US)

scratch comma   punctuation mark in form of oblique stroke

screamer   slang for exclamation mark

screen	see 'halftone screen'
screen angle	angle at which halftone screen is arranged; whenever two or more halftones are to overprint, to avoid screen clash (see below)
screen clash	undesirable pattern resulting from overprinting of two or more halftones at unsuitable screen angles (see also 'moiré'):

screen (process) printing	one in which squeegee forces ink through fine screen of fabric or metal to which is fixed a stencil:

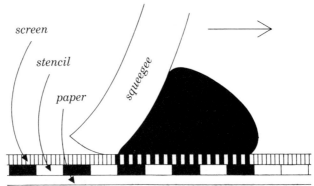

photographic, rather than cut, stencils are now common, and high speed, high quality screen printing is now possible

screen tester	device which, if laid on printed halftone and rotated until symmetrical moiré pattern (qv) is produced, will indicate screen size
screenless photolitho	process using troughs or peaks of grained aluminium plate as image receptors in positive or negative workings respectively, instead of photochemical halftone screen
script (type)	typeface designed in imitation of writing done with pen or brush,

152

often having characters made to fit closely as in joined writing:

$\mathscr{A}\,\mathscr{B}\ \mathscr{C}abcde$

scumming   in lithography, fault in which water-accepting layer is worn away from non-image areas, giving dirty-looking impression

secondary colour   one resulting from combination of two 'primary colours' (qv)

section   sheet of paper folded into four or more pages to make into gathered or insetted book; also known as 'signature', especially in US

section mark   type character indicating beginning of new section; also used as fourth order of 'reference marks' (qv) for footnotes

section-sewn book   one in which gathered sections are secured by sewn thread (see 'binding methods')

sector chart   same as 'pie chart' (qv)

see-through   degree to which image on underlying surface can be seen through sheet of paper

selective focussing   in photography, using lens at full, or near full, aperture to focus on particular subject throwing background and/or foreground out-of-focus:

focussed at 60cm, f4 aperture   *focussed at 120cm, f4 aperture*

Selectric   trade name for popular make of direct impression, or 'strike-on', composing machine

self-cover	book cover made of same material as leaves of book
self-ends	'endpapers' (qv) which are part of first and last sections of book
semantics	see 'semiotic(s)'
semaphore code	one devised for signalling by movements of arms, human or mechanical:

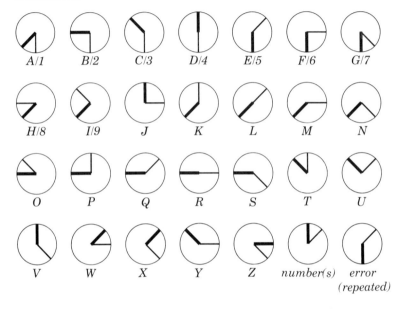

semiotic(s), semiology	study of nature and use of signs, whether spoken, gesticulated, written, printed or constructed; divided into three levels, syntactics (relations between signs), semantics (relations between signs and things they refer to) and pragmatics (relations between signs and those who use them):

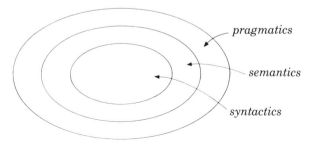

separate (as noun)	same as 'offprint' (qv)
separation artwork	separate drawings for each colour of a colour illustration, usually by means of opaque base artwork and transparent overlays keyed together by 'register marks' (qv)
sepia toning	in photography, treating bromide prints with special chemicals (toners) to produce brown image
series	see 'type series'
serif	finishing strokes or terminals at ends of type characters
serigraphy	another name for 'silk-screen process' (qv)
set	width of piece of type; in Monotype machine composition, all characters (including spaces) have 'set' width, expressed in units, which are not standard dimensions, like points, but are related to proportion of typeface design; widest character is divided into 18 equal units, other characters are allocated unit values in proportion:

set and hold	instruction to printer to set an item and hold it for future use, as, for example, an obituary
set-off	still-wet impression making mark on adjacent sheet just after printing; sometimes (confusingly) called 'offset'
set solid	type which is set without leading or other additional interlinear spacing
set-square	triangular drawing implement made of transparent plastic
set theory	study of relations of sets to each other and to subjects within them (see also 'Venn diagram')
set-up key	in film animation, instruction given to camera operator on camera movements and 'field sizes' (qv)

sewn book	any book secured with sewn thread
sexto, 6to	cut or folded sheet which is one sixth of basic sheet size
shade (of colour)	result of admixing small amounts of black with basic hue
shaded letter	'outline letter' (qv) with shadow effect running down one side of strokes, thus:

SPECIMEN

shank (of type)	main part of piece of type by which it is raised to printing height (see 'type')
sheet	whole piece of paper, flat or folded; there are many basic sheet sizes in printing
sheet-fed	printing machine in which paper is fed one sheet at a time as distinct from 'reel-/web-fed' (qv)
sheet proof	one taken from a forme; also called an 'imposed proof'
sheet stock	printed sheets held in store for binding up
sheet work	form of imposition in which pages on one side of sheet are in one forme and those for other side are in another forme; see also 'half-sheet work'
sheetwise	most common printing method, in which sheet is printed first on one side, then on the other, to produce complete section as distinct from 'half-sheet work' (qv)
shelfback (of book)	same as 'back' (qv)
shilling mark	old name for 'solidus' (qv), 'oblique stroke' or 'slash'
short and	same as 'ampersand' (qv)
short ink	one which tends to be crumbly and cannot be rolled into thin film
shoulder (of type)	non-printing area surrounding face of type, and from which it rises (see 'type')

156

shoulder note	one which is set in side margin at head of paragraph
showprint	same as 'release print' (qv)
show-through	degree to which image on reverse of sheet shows through paper
shriek	slang for 'exclamation mark'
shrink-wrapping	in packaging, application of very thin, usually transparent, film over product and shrinking it to sealed, air-tight fit
shutter, between-the-lens	camera shutter which opens by means of pivoting, interleaved blades
shutter, focal plane	camera shutter, consisting of two blinds on either side of narrow slit, travelling across film on rollers; slit varies in width according to exposure time
SI unit	unit of measure conforming to *Système Internationale*
SIAD	initials of Society of Industrial Artists and Designers (UK), founded in 1930; well meaning but somewhat ineffectual affair which has neither exclusivity of professional body like Law Society nor bargaining power of trade union
sic	Latin for 'thus', used within parentheses to confirm accuracy of preceding word, usually because of unorthodox spelling
side-heading	heading in side margin at top of page or paragraph
side stab/stitch	to secure book by means of wire forced through side close to back
sign	in communication studies, any means whereby one human, animal or plant seeks to affect behaviour or condition of another by communication; 'sign-types' are those universals (such as letters of alphabet) which are drawn on to produce 'sign-events', physical embodiment of sign-types (such as speech or piece of writing)
signature	letter or number printed at bottom of first page of each section of book, to ensure correct sequence; also (especially in US), synonym for 'section'
silhouette halftone	one in which the outline follows the shape of some part of subject of illustration (same as 'cut-out')

silkscreen process	traditional form of 'screen process' (qv) in which screen is made of silk, still used for fine art prints; also known as 'serigraphy'
single-lens reflex	see 'camera types'
sixteen-mo, 16mo	cut or folded sheet which is one sixteenth of basic sheet size
sixteen-sheet	poster size of 120 × 80in (305 × 203cm)
skip-framing	in cinefilm, deleting given number of film frames from shot at regular intervals, to reduce running time or speed up action
skyline (of newspaper)	banner headline running above nameplate
slab-serif	typeface with markedly square-ended serifs which may or may not be 'bracketed' (qv):

ABCDEFGHIJKLMN
The bank recognizes

slash	same as 'oblique' and 'solidus' (qv); more common in US
slide binder	see 'plastic grip/slide spine'
slip	long, narrow strip of paper used for 'galley proof' (qv)
slip case	container for book or set of books, made so that spine is left visible
slip-sheeting	US term for 'interleaving' (qv)
slip page	proof made up on 'slip' (qv) but separated out as one page
slip proof	same as 'galley proof' (qv) but may also be taken to mean 'slip page'
sloped roman	correct term for many typefaces which are generally known as italics even though they are not 'cursive' (qv)
SLR	initials of 'single lens reflex' (camera)
slug	line of type cast as continuous piece on line composing machine

slur	fault in printing caused by movement during making of impression
slurred dot (type)	termination of certain characters, resembling distorted dot:

𝑘

small caps (abb: sc, s caps)	smaller version of capital letters, about same height as x-height of lower case letters
small face	smaller of two sizes available on same body of typeface
snoot	in photographic lighting, cone-shaped device fitted in front of spotlight to give very narrow light beam
soft (paper)	in photography, one giving low contrast image
soft copy	in photocomposition, display of keyboarded copy on VDU
soft cover	one not made from stiff board
software	term to describe programs and other operating instructions for computer, as distinct from 'hardware' (qv)
solidus	oblique stroke, thus / used to denote alternatives, ratios and fractions; also called 'slash' or 'oblique'
solus position	advertisement space on page where there is no other advertisement
sort	single piece of type; a 'special sort' is one not usually included in fount, but available on order
SP	initials of 'station point' (qv)
spaceband	wedge device used in mechanical type composition to provide variable word spacing
spec (pron: speck or spess)	slang for 'specification', which is definition of data and procedures required to execute task
special sort	type character not normally included in 'fount' (qv)
specimen page	one set up and proofed to show effect of proposed layout style

speed-rating (of film)　　see 'film speed'

spine　　that edge of book at which leaves and covers are secured; also called 'back' and 'backbone' (see 'book')

spiral binder　　one in which leaves are secured by spiral wire wound through small, pre-drilled holes; sometimes, but totally inaccurately, applied to plastic comb binder (see 'binding methods'):

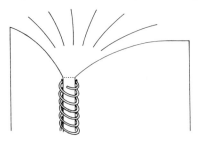

spirit duplicating　　simple planographic printing process for up to 100 copies by means of aniline dye transfer printing onto plain sheets moistened with spirit solvent

splayed 'M'　　one like this:

splicer　　in cinefilm, mechanical device used to hold two pieces of film in proper position for splicing by means of tape, cement or hot-splice

split dash/rule　　one like this:

split duct/fountain　　device to divide ink supply so that two or three colours may be printed at once on same sheet; also used to obtain blending of colours

split fraction　　same as 'piece fraction' (qv)

spoils, spoilage	sheets which are badly printed and so not included in delivered quantity of job; printers usually allow for this by printing 'overs'
spotmeter	in photography, light meter with very limited angle of view, such as are incorporated in many reflex cameras; measures light value only of that portion of scene central to view
spotting	delicate form of photo-retouching, solely concerned with eliminating small processing blemishes from prints; almost always an essential finishing task when making first quality prints
spraygun	same as 'airbrush' (qv)
spread	pair of facing pages, left-hand and right-hand; often considered as design unit even though pages may be printed in different sections
square-back book	one in which wrappered, drawn-on or cased cover forms flat spine that is not 'rounded and backed' (qv)
square-serif	same as 'slab-serif' (qv)
squared-up (halftone)	normal form of halftone, in which edges are straight and rectangular
squares (of book)	bookbinders' term for overhanging edges of 'cased book' (qv)
squealer	slang for exclamation mark
SRA paper sizes	see 'A, B and C Series'
S/S	abbreviation for 'same size' (qv)
stand-alone	electronic unit to which input must be supplied from outside, as distinct from one linked directly to central computer or operator
stand camera	see 'camera types'
standard aspect ratio	see 'aspect ratio'
standing type/matter	composed type matter kept for possible reprint rather than being melted down or 'dissed' (qv)
starburst filter	in photography, attachment to camera lens which produces 'starburst' effect from point source of strong light

star graph	one in which values are plotted as radii from point of origin; also known as 'rose diagram' and 'vector diagram':

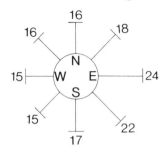

stat	abbreviation for 'photostat' (qv)
station point (abb: SP)	in 'perspective projections' (qv), imagined position of eye of observer viewing object
STD	initials of 'Society of Typographic Designers' (UK)
stem	main vertical, or near vertical, part of type character
stencil duplication	same as 'mimeography' (qv)
step-and-repeat	photomechanical method of producing multiple images from one original by means of special step-and-repeat machine
step index	one in which steps are cut out of foredge for greater ease of reference; sometimes called 'cut-in' index:

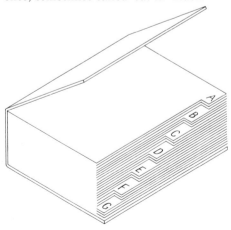

stereotype, stereo	duplicate letterpress plate cast from mould
stet	Latin for 'let it stand': instruction to leave some part of proof as it was before previous correction was made
stiff-leaves	endpapers (qv) which are glued to whole of first and last leaves in book, rather than just being 'tipped-on'
still-frame	in use of videotape recorder (VTR), repetitive playback of one picture, equivalent to 'freeze-frame' or 'stop-frame' in cinefilm
stock	any material to be used for printing on
stone	surface (once made of stone) on which letterpress formes are imposed before being transferred to bed of press
stone hand	in letterpress printing, one who arranges and secures composed type matter and plates in correct order for printing
stop bath	in photography, dilute acid solution used to arrest development before fixing
stop-cylinder press	'cylinder press' (qv) in which cylinder remains stationary whilst printing bed is returned after being moved out of contact for inking, as distinct from 'two-revolution press'
stop-frame	operating mode in cinefilm whereby each frame is exposed separately; used in film animation
stop-motion	same as 'freeze-frame' (qv)
storyboard	set of preliminary sketches showing how cinefilm or TV sequence is intended to develop and give idea of timing and content without going into detail
strap	subsidiary headline placed over main headline of newspaper or periodical feature
strawboard	one made from straw pulp; used for making covers of cased books
stress (type)	direction implied by position of thickest part of rounded characters
stretch-printing	in cinefilm, printing every other film frame twice, especially in order to convert film shot at one speed for projection in another

163

strike-on composition	same as 'direct impression' (qv)
strike-through	penetration of printing ink through sheet from one side to other
striker	slang for exclamation mark
stripping up together	combining two or more negatives or positives for photomechanical reproduction
stripping up as one	as above, but superimposing them to produce single new image; also known, especially in US, as 'surprinting' or 'double-burning'
studio camera	see 'camera types'
style of house	set of rules used by printer or publisher in typesetting and make-up (see also 'house style')
s/u	abbreviation for 'squared-up' (qv)
sub-editor	one who assists an editor in preparing copy for printing
subject to correction	important qualification to an 'OK to print'
subscript	same as 'inferior numeral or figure' (qv)
substance of . . . (abb: s/o . . .)	way of measuring paper by weight of ream of specified size; now superceded in UK by 'g/m^2' (qv)
subtractive colour mixing	reproducing colour by mixing or superimposing inks, paints or dyes, as distinct from 'additive colour mixing' (qv); in effect, all applications of ink, etc, to surface such as white paper subtract (absorb) some portion of white light reflected from it:

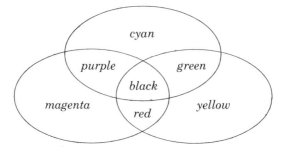

subsidiaries	see 'end-matter'

substrate	in photography, material (eg: celluloid) used as carrier of sensitized emulsion; in printing, material (eg: paper, board) used to print on
supercalendered paper	glossy (but not coated) paper produced by being passed through 'supercalender' rolls under great pressure
super-caster	Monotype machine for casting display size type, spaces, borders, leads, rules and ornaments
super ellipse	one of range of regular, closed curves devised by Danish mathematician Piet Hein in 1959; best described as ellipse trying to turn into rectangle:

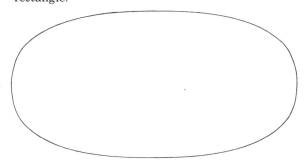

superior numeral (figure) or letter	small character set above level of normal characters of typeface (eg: $4^3 = 64$)
supers	in cinefilm and TV, lettering or graphics superimposed on film
superscript	same as 'superior numeral or letter' (qv)
surprinting	1) in photomechanical reproduction, combining two or more negatives to produce single new image; similar to 'stripping-up-as-one' (qv) but with implication that extra negative stage may be involved (mainly US term) 2) US term for 'overprinting' (qv)
swash character	one with emphatic flourish, thus:

$$\mathcal{ABDEFGHI}$$

(note that 'J' was originally swash form of 'I')

swell (of book)	extra bulking at back of book as result of sewing; reduced by 'smashing' in bookbinder's press
swelled dash/rule	one like this: ————————————
symbol	any figure devised and accepted as representation of some object, idea, activity, process, relationship or combination of these
sync-sound	in cinefilm and TV, synchronization of sound with images
synecdoche	see 'pars pro toto'
syntactics	see 'semiotics(s)'

T (= time)	in photography, setting on camera shutter for use in making long exposures; when exposure release is pressed, shutter is opened and remains open until exposure release is pressed again
T square	ruler with cross piece at one end, used in conjunction with drawing board when drawing parallel lines
tab index	one in which divisions are indicated by projecting tabs on foredge:

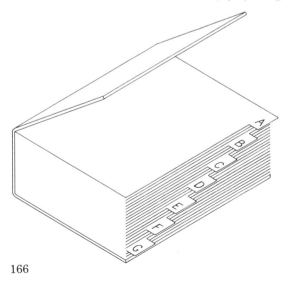

tabbing	1) arranging copy (typewritten or typeset) in multi-columnar pattern within set measure; colloquialism for 'tabulation' (qv) 2) forming projecting portions to edges of book so as to make 'tab index' (qv)
tablet	same as 'digitizing pad' (qv)
tabulation	arranging information in list, or table form
tachistoscope	optical instrument which reveals chosen image at measured brief intervals to allow observation of viewer response
tail	bottom of book (qv); also known as 'foot', especially in US
tail margin	see 'page'
take	1) portion of whole typesetting job allocated to one compositor 2) in cinefilm, single shooting of one scene
take back	instruction to printer on proof: take line or lines of type back to previous page or column
take in	instruction to printer on manuscript or proof to take in added copy
take over	instruction to printer on proof: take line or lines of type over to next column or subsequent page
taking lens	on twin lens camera, lens which throws image onto film, as distinct from viewing lens
tear sheet	file copy of editorial content or advertisement torn from periodical
tele-	prefix meaning 'at a distance'
telecommunication	sending or receiving signals, sounds or messages of any kind by television, radio, telegraph, telephone or other electromagnetic means
Telecopier	trade name for device which transmits graphic information over ordinary telephone line
teleprinter	typewriter-like device using continuous stationery, used to communicate with similar device over 'telex' (qv) link or as input to/output from computer

teletext	technique for transmitting information in which encoded data are sent with broadcast TV signal or along telephone lines, then decoded and displayed by special electronics in domestic TV receiver
Teletypesetter (TTS)	trade name for device producing perforated tape for use in certain typecasting machines
teletypewriter	same as 'teleprinter' (qv)
telex	telegraphic system by which messages are sent from one teleprinter to another over public telephone network (term derived from *tele*printer *ex*change)
tertiary colour	one resulting from combination of two 'secondary colours' (qv)
text letter	yet another (confusing) synonym for 'black letter' (qv)
text type	any type which may be used for continuous text, up to 14pt
thermocopy	one achieved by heat as against light (photocopy)
thermography	technique in which heat-treated ink image produces raised effect (note: not complete printing process)
Thermo-Fax	trade name for well-known make of thermocopy
thick (space)	commonly used word space in handsetting: $^1/_3$ em of set
thin (space)	commonly used word space in handsetting: $^1/_5$ em of set
third angle projection	see 'multiview projections'
thirtytwo-mo, 32mo	cut or folded sheet which is one thirtysecond of a basic sheet size
thirtytwo-sheet poster	poster size 120 × 160in (3048 × 4065mm)
threadless binding	same as 'perfect binding' (qv) and 'unsewn binding'
three-colour process	similar to 'four-colour process' (qv) except that there is no separate black printing; also called 'trichromatic system'
three-point perspective	see 'perspective projections'
throw-out	same as 'fold-out' (qv)

throw up	instruction to printer to emphasise word, phrase, sentence or para-graph
thumb index	one in which thumb-sized chunks are cut out of foredge for greater ease of reference:

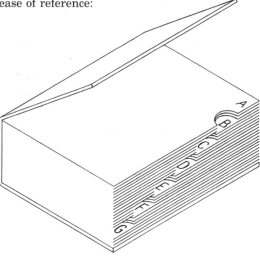

thumbnail	miniature sketch design or layout
tied letter	same as 'ligature' (qv)
tilde	see 'accented (diacritical) signs'
time exposure	in photography, lengthy exposure of film – anything from few seconds to several hours – which may be for purpose of obtaining blurred movement' or because light from subject is too weak
time-lapse photography	in cinefilm, method in which prolonged process, such as plant growth, is photographed in sequence of single exposures and then projected at normal speed
tint (of colour)	result of admixing small amounts of white with basic hue
tint plate	one used to print colour background to type, line or halftone matter
tipping in/on	attaching single leaf to section of book or periodical by means of strip of paste or glue at back edge; see also 'guarding'
title page	that page of book carrying title, author and publisher

title sheet/section	first sheet or section of book, usually having no signature, so that second part is printed as 'B' or '2' signature, indicating that there is one preceding it
titling	fount of capitals only, cast on body having very short 'beard' (qv), since there are no descenders
tone separation	same as 'posterization (qv)
toners	in photography, chemicals used to convert black tones of bromide print into another colour, eg: sepia
topography	science of representing features of any district in detail, as on map
topology	branch of mathematics concerned with contiguity and relative position, rather than with congruence and dimension
tracing materials	used for drawings of which direct reproduction copies are required; following types are available: detail paper (cheap, not very translucent, tears easily); natural tracing paper (cheap. translucent but tears easily); prepared tracing paper (more expensive, more durable but less translucent); tracing cloth (expensive, very durable, reasonably translucent but needs preparation before use); acetate-based (expensive, very translucent but tears easily and becomes brittle); polyester-based (very expensive, very translucent, very durable, dimensionally stable)
tracking	in cinefilm and TV, movement of camera along track in relation to subject:

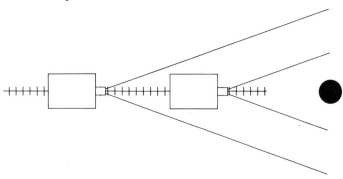

trade mark	word, words or graphic device intended to denote relationship between goods or services to which it is applied and proprietor of mark; in UK trade mark must be registered with Patent Office
trade setter	one who sets and proofs type for others and does not print in quantity
tranny	slang for 'transparency'
transfer lettering	image of type or other lettering which is transferred from transparent backing sheet by pressure; also called 'dry transfer'
transparency (as noun)	photographic image, usually coloured and positive, on transparent film; may be used either as basis for photomechanical reproduction, for backlit display or for slide projection
transferring (lithography)	drawing or impressing inked image onto special coated paper and transferring it thence to lithographic printing surface
transitional	class of typefaces dating from mid-18th century, having somewhat finer serifs and hairlines than 'old-face' but not to extent of 'modern':

ABDE most pages

travelling matte	see 'matte'
triangle	US term for 'set-square' (qv)
trichromatic system	colour reproduction by three-colour, instead of four-colour, separation; same as 'three-colour process' (qv)
trigram, trigraph	combination of three letters which represent one sound, as in 'eau' of b*eau*
trim marks	those incorporated on sheet when printed, to show how job is to be trimmed, and which are not visible in printed result
trimetric projection	see 'axonometric projections'
trimming	final cutting to size of printed job by guillotine
trs	abbreviation for 'transpose'; instructions on manuscript or proof to

transpose character, word, phrase or sentence

true small cap	type character intended for use as small cap, as distinct from one adapted for purpose, either by using cap from small type size or (in photocomposition) by photographic reduction from cap of same size
TTL meter	exposure meter situated within camera body, measuring light passing through lens (TTL = through-the-lens)
TTS	1) abbreviation for 'Teletypesetter' (qv) 2) initials of 'True-to-Scale': trade name for limited quantity reproduction process using gelatine plate; especially suitable for architectural and engineering drawings when accuracy and stability are needed
turned commas	same as 'inverted commas' (qv)
turned-over cover	one with extended flaps on foredge, similar to 'book jacket' (qv)
tungsten film	colour film for use in artificial light emitting from tungsten bulbs
tungsten halogen lamp	photographic light source consisting of special form of tungsten lamp with trace of a halogen gas, smaller and brighter than conventional lamp; sometimes called 'quartz-iodine' lamp, though it may not contain either quartz or iodine
turnaround document	one which is encoded via computer so that it can be returned after use by human; example is retail tag which can be read by retailer, buyer and stock control computer
turn up (type)	to reverse a type feet uppermost, to indicate that required character is not yet available
twelve-mo, 12mo	cut or folded sheet which is one twelfth of basic sheet size
twin-lens reflex	see 'camera types'
twin-wire paper	that which is made from machine producing paper which has no 'wire-mark' and so is smooth on both sides
two-point perspective	see 'perspective drawings'
two-revolution press	cylinder press (qv) which revolves continuously (as distinct from 'stop-cylinder press') and makes two revolutions to each impression

172

two-up, three-up, etc.	two items of print, or same one repeated, printing simultaneously on same side of sheet
type	1) piece of metal of standard height having raised image of character or characters on its upper face, assembled with other pieces to form line which is printed by letterpress (relief) process:

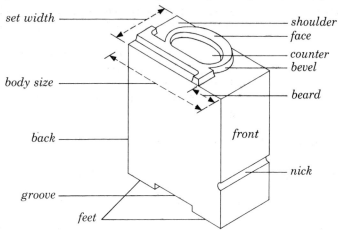

2) images obtained by printing from this metal
3) images obtained from composition systems which do not use metal type (eg: photocomposition)

type area	specified area of page or trimmed sheet which contains body of text matter and illustrations (see 'page')
type family	all variants (eg: light, medium, bold, condensed, expanded) of all sizes of given type design
type-height	standard height of type from bed to printing surface: 0.918 inches in UK and US; also called 'height-to-paper'
type mark-up	typesetting instructions to compositor on manuscript or typescript, accompanied by general specification
type scale/gauge	rule marked in ems and points, and often also in inches and millimetres, for use in layout, imposition and proof correction; also called 'line gauge' and 'pica rule'
type series	those designs and sizes of typeface referred to by manufacturer by same series number

type-to-type	same as 'fold-to-print' (qv)
type specimen sheet	one giving full alphabets, figures and signs, with some text settings, of particular typeface
typeface	printing surface of piece of type; by extension and more commonly, design of any particular set of types
typeface classification	several attempts have been made to evolve typeface classification systems, notably by Maximilien Vox in France (1954) and Deutscher Normenausschuss in Germany (1964); most recent is British Standard 2961: 1967 which is based on Vox system and lists classes of typefaces as follows:

humanist, formerly 'Venetian' (qv);
garalde, formerly 'old face' (qv) or 'old style';
transitional (qv);
didone, formerly 'modern' (qv);
slab-serif (qv);
lineale, formerly 'sans-serif', which divides into:
   grotesque;
   neo-grotesque;
   geometric;
humanist;
glyphic (qv);
script (qv);
graphic (qv);
and compounds of the above, eg: humanist/garalde

typewriter faces	there are two standard sizes: 'elite' (having twelve characters to the inch) and 'pica' (having ten characters to the inch), names also applied to the most common designs in these sizes:

```
This is a specimen of Elite type
This is a specimen of Pica type
```

typo	slang for 'typographic error'; can refer to either typewriting or type-setting mistake (US term)
typographer	confusing: in UK this term is often used to mean 'typographic designer' but in US it means 'one who sets type' (ie: compositor)
typography	originally (and still to some extent in US) art and technique of

174

working with type; in UK it has come to mean, specifically, layout
of typeset and accompanying graphic matter for reproduction

u

UDC	initials of 'Universal Decimal Classification': system of classifying areas of knowledge developed as extension of 'Dewey Decimal Classification' (qv)
ultra-violet	near-visible waves in 'electromagnetic spectrum' (qv) which can affect some photographic materials and which may need to be absorbed by filters so as to reduce haze
umlaut	see 'accented (diacritical) signs'
unit system	in machine composition of type, method of relating character widths to unit measurements, originally developed by Monotype; units are not standard dimensions but vary according to 'set' (qv)
Universal Copyright Convention 1952	agreement between signatory countries giving protection for copyright proprietor of text, photograph, illustration, movie, work of art, etc, providing work carries proper copyright notice consisting of © symbol, name of copyright proprietor and year of publication
universal developer	in photography, one which can be used either for film or print development, depending on strength of solution
Universal Product Code	see 'bar code'
unjustified	taken to mean type lines which line up horizontally on one side and are ragged on other; strictly speaking, all lines of type are 'justified' (qv) but this misnomer is now hallowed by use
unjustified tape	in photocomposition, tape output of 'non-counting keyboard' in which operator makes no end-of-line decisions about justification and word-breaks; also called 'idiot tape'
unsewn binding	same as 'perfect binding' (qv) and 'threadless binding'
UPC	initials of 'Universal Product Code' (see 'bar code')

upper-case	another name for 'capitals' (qv) deriving from traditional position of that case containing capital letters, small caps and figures; most often used in expression 'upper-and-lower-case', meaning upper-case for initial letters of sentences and proper names, lower-case for rest
uprating film	in photography, exposing film at speed and stop applicable to higher 'ASA' (qv) or 'DIN' rating, then giving it increased development to compensate for under-exposure; useful technique where lighting conditions are very poor
upstroke (of type)	lighter stroke in type character, deriving from upward movement of pen in calligraphy:

useful redundancy	see 'redundancy'
u/lc, U&LC	abbreviations for 'upper-and-lower-case'
u/v, U/V	initials of 'ultra-violet' (qv)

vacuum forming	shaping thin plastic sheeting by means of vacuum:

 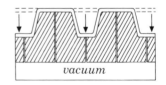

vacuum

vacuum (printing) frame	illuminated printing frame used to make process negatives and positives; vacuum provides best contact between surfaces
value (of colour)	degree of lightness or darkness of colour in relation to neutral grey scale

Van Dyke print	photocopy in dark brown colour, used as proof; also known as 'brownprint'
vanishing point (abb: VP)	in 'perspective projections' (qv), point at which all parallel lines which are also parallel to ground plane converge on horizon
vapour diazo	same as 'ammonia duplication process' (qv)
Varityper	trade name for make of typewriter specially designed for direct impression (qv) type composition
varnish	transparent liquid which can be added to ink or overprinted to give high-gloss finish
VDT	initials of 'visual display terminal' device incorporating keyboard, logic system and cathode ray tube (CRT), and connected to computer; used to display alphanumeric or graphic information stored in computer, also to key in queries so that result of interrogation may be viewed on screen
VDU	initials of 'visual display unit', cathode ray tube (CRT) which may be used as part of 'VDT' (qv) or as 'stand-alone' information device
vector	generally, any quantity having both magnitude and direction and expressed by straight line of given length; more specifically, those line increments from which some types of computer-generated graphics displays are formed:

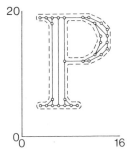

vector diagram	see 'star graph'
vehicle (of ink)	carrier of ink pigment, all or mostly composed of varnish and solvent

velox	halftone-screened photoprint of continuous-tone subject, suitable for inclusion on camera ready artwork along with line copy
venetian (of typeface)	early form of roman which retains sloping bar to 'e' from calligraphic origin and has less variation between thick and thin strokes:

PAST the

Venn diagram	one using circles, ovals or other closed figures to illustrate sets, named after John Venn, who used them from 1880; also known as 'Euler circles' after Leonhard Euler, who used them in 1770 (though they appear to have been invented by Johann Christoph Sturm in 1661):

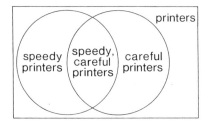

verso	any left-hand page of book; one which is even-numbered
vertex (pl: vertices)	in geometry, meeting-point of lines that form an angle;
VET	initials of 'visual editing terminal'; visual display terminal with specific editing function
vide	Latin for 'see'; used in footnotes to direct reader to particular book, chapter or passage
video editor	in photocomposition, editing device incorporating 'CRT' (qv)
video layout system (VLS)	CRT system used for layout planning prior to photocomposition (see also 'area composition')
video monitor	in videotape recording (VTR), device for viewing recording, at moment of shooting or afterwards when editing; like TV receiver without tuning controls

178

videotape	magnetic recording tape used in recording TV signals, both sound and vision
videotex	alternate name for 'teletext' (qv) recommended by some authorities
view camera	one having ground glass screen at back for viewing and focusing at image plane
Viewdata	interactive information service devised by UK Post Office, using normal telephone line as transmission channel and adapted TV set as display unit, with similar format to 'Ceefax' and 'Oracle' (qqv); marketed in UK as 'Prestel'
vignetted halftone	one in which edges are gradually shaded off into background:

visual	a representation to show intended result of print job; may be a quick sketch or 'presentation visual' (qv)
visual display terminal	see 'VDT'
visual editing terminal	see 'VET'
visualizer	illuminated device which produces enlarged or reduced image for use in visual; may also be used as simple photoprinting enlarger
viz	abbreviation of *videlicet*, Latin for 'namely', used in footnotes
VLS	initials of 'video layout system' (qv)
VP	initials of 'vanishing point' (qv)
VTR	initials of '*video tape recorder*'

W

wallet envelope	one with quadrilateral, as distinct from, triangular, flap
wallet-fold	same as 'gate-fold' (see 'folding methods') but may be applied more particularly to wallet-fold cover
wash up	in printing, cleaning of rollers, ink ducts and press before another colour can be printed
watermark	faint design imparted into certain uncoated papers when they are being made, to identify mills they come from
web	reel or ribbon of paper as formed on paper-making machine
web-fed	used of printing machine in which paper is fed from web or reel rather than from flat sheets
wedge-serif	typeface with triangular serifs, also known as 'latin':

ABCDEFabcdefgh

weight (of type-face)	comparative strength of appearance of any typeface
wet-on-wet	printing technique in which one colour is printed on another whilst first one is still wet
wf	abbreviation of 'wrong fount': correction to proof indicating that character from another typeface has been used in error
wheel graph	see 'pie graph'
white line	in typesetting, space between lines of type equal to that left if one line of type is omitted
widow	last line of typeset paragraph consisting of one word only
wild cel	in film animation, one not fixed to register pegs and thus able to move about freely under rostrum camera
wild track	in cinefilm, sound recorded without matching camera shot

window	1) in photolitho processing, hole cut in 'flat' (qv) for insertion of negative material which is to print down on plate 2) in typesetting, another word for 'river' (qv)
wipe	in cinefilm and TV editing, one shot moving in from side, top or bottom as viewed, progressively replacing previous shot
wire-photo	technique of transmitting photograph (or any other pictorial form) by means of photo-electric cells; also called 'phototelegraphy'
wire-side	that side of some uncoated papers (such as 'antiques') which shows a 'wire-mark', as distinct from 'felt-side'
wire-stitch/stab	to secure book by forcing wire through back of insetted work or side of gathered work
woodcut	relief printing block in which non-printing portions are cut away by knife along grain of wood, giving strong, simple black line:

wood-engraving	relief printed block similar to woodcut except that special engraving tools are used, cutting on end grain of wood to achieve finer effect:

woodfree	said of paper which is free of mechanical wood pulp, using chemical pulp instead; known in US as 'freesheet'
word-breaking	splitting words at end of line of type to avoid gappy wordspacing
word processor	special typewriter linked with recording devices such as magnetic tape, to provide for revision, updating, storing and rapid playback; usually taken to mean equipment used in office by secretary/typist
word spacing	in machine composition other than linecasting, word spacing conforms to 'unit system' (qv); in hand composition, word spaces are provided in the following widths:

em quad   *en quad*   *thick*   *middle*   *thin*

work and turn	to print 'forme' (qv) on one side of sheet, turn it over from left to right and print same forme on reverse, thus producing two identical half-sheets; most common type of 'half-sheet work':

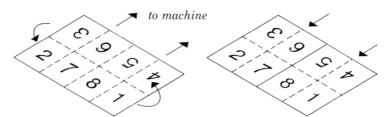

work and tumble	similar to 'work and turn', except that sheet is turned over from 'gripper edge' (qv) to back, instead of from left to right:

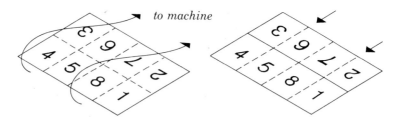

work and twist	to print forme on one side of sheet, then turn it round (not over) and print again from same forme (particularly suited to work involving crossed rules):

182

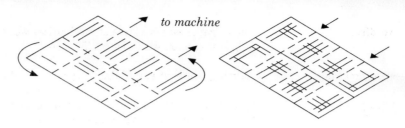

to machine

work print	in cinefilm, same as 'cutting copy' (qv); more common in US
work up	in letterpress, type space which has been accidentally pushed up
working	in printing, one operation on printing machine, whether of inking, stamping, creasing, perforating or embossing
wove paper	uncoated paper which has an even, unpatterned look-through
wrap-around plate	letterpress plate which wraps around cylinder, similar to offset-litho plate
wrap-round, wraparound	small printing section (4pp or 8pp) wrapped around another section in gathered work (see 'gathering'; also known as 'outset'
wrap-around press	letterpress machine using curved printing plate wrapped around cylinder
wrappering cover	attaching cover to paperback book or periodical by glueing to spine only (see also 'drawing-on cover')
wrong-reading	see 'reverse reading'

X

x-axis	horizontal axis in 'coordinate graph' (qv)
x-height	mean height of lower case characters which have neither ascenders nor descenders:

mean line ⋯⋯ ⋯⋯ ⎯ *x-height*

base line ⋯⋯ OXy ⋯⋯

183

xerography	printing process in which image is projected onto plate, causing electrostatic charge already imparted to be discharged where light falls, thus allowing applied coating of resinous powder to adhere only to uncharged areas and then transfer to paper; also known as 'photostatic' or 'dry copying' process:

surface is electrostatically charged

image projected onto surface dissipates charge in illuminated areas

applied 'toner' powder adheres to areas which retain charge and is then fixed by heat

xylography	posh name for wood-block printing

yapp binding	binding form in which limp cover overlaps leaves of book (after William Yapp, who devised it for his pocket bibles)
y-axis	vertical axis in 'coordinate graph' (qv)

Z

zenithal projections	group of projections of Earth in which plane of projection is assumed to touch globe at single point, as distinct from 'cylindrical' or 'conic' projections (qqv); typical zenithal projections are:

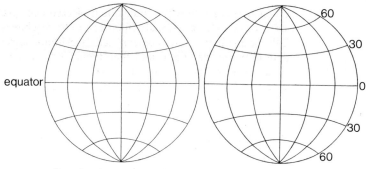

Lambert's equatorial zenithal equal area

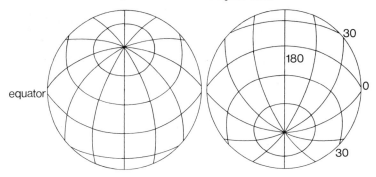

Lambert's oblique zenithal equal area

zig-zag book   one made as continuous, concertina fold, usually printed one side only; may be stitched at back or left unstitched so that it may be opened up, either for display or to reveal printed reverse:

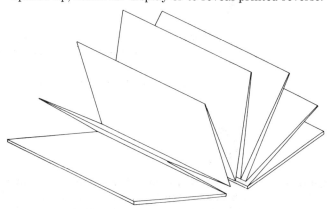

bibliophiles call zig-zag book formed from manuscript roll an 'orihon'

zinco, zincograph	letterpress line plate made of zinc
zoom lens	variable-focus camera lens; way of having several lenses in one
zooming	in cinefilm and TV, using zoom lens to decrease or increase 'field area' (qv) during shooting, so that camera appears to approach or retreat from subject (see also 'tracking'):

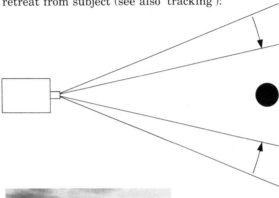

effect of 'zooming-in'   *effect of 'tracking-in' for comparison*

Bibliography

All dates shown are for the most recent edition, with preference given to paperback editions, signified by 'pb'

■ ■ ■ Essential   ■ ■ Important but not essential   ■ Useful

History of design: general

Banham P R
■ ■ ■ *Theory and design in the first machine age*
Architectural Press, London, 1960
Brilliant and stimulating analysis of design revolution which took place in first thirty years of this century, from which current thinking and practice have derived; should be read as follow-on from *Pioneers of modern design* (see below)

Bayer H, Gropius W and Gropius I (eds)
■ ■ ■ *Bauhaus 1919–1928*
Branford, Boston, 1959
Account by its founder-director, his wife and one of his famous colleagues, of development of most influential design school of this century

Pevsner N
■ ■ ■ *Pioneers of modern design*
Penguin, Harmondsworth, 1960pb
Masterly survey of growth of Modern Movement in design and architecture from mid-nineteenth century; first written 1939 but fully revised since

History of printing, graphics, typography and photography

Ades D
■ ■ *Photomontage*
Thames and Hudson, London, 1976pb
Very useful compendium of annotated illustrations with helpful, if brief, introduction

187

Gernsheim H and Gernsheim A

■ ■ ■ *A concise history of photography*
Thames and Hudson, London, 1965pb
Authors trace evolution of photographic techniques and examine
both artistic and social implications of medium; splendid selection
of illustrations, dating from 1826 to 1960

Gerstner K and Kutter M

■ ■ *The new graphic art*
Niggli, Teufen, 1959
Clear, thoughtful selection of illustrations of key works in
development of graphic design from late nineteenth century to
1950's; runs risk of being used as a crib, but worth it for rarity of
many of illustrations and for informative annotations

Spencer H

■ ■ ■ *Pioneers of modern typography*
Lund Humphries, London, 1969pb
Meticulous teasing-out of roots of modern typography, which were
nourished more from painting, poetry and architecture rather than
conventional printing; superb illustrations

Twyman M

■ ■ ■ *Printing from 1770–1970*
Eyre and Spottiswoode, London, 1970
Thorough, well illustrated and enjoyable

Photography and film animation

Hedgecoe J

■ ■ ■ *Photographer's handbook*
Ebury Press, London, 1977
Profusely illustrated work of reference, particularly useful to
graphic designers; not cheap but worth every penny

Madsen R

■ ■ ■ *Animated film: concepts, methods, uses*
Focal Press, London and New York, 1969
Excellent, authoritative guide with clear, helpful illustrations

Maré E de

■ ■ *Photography*
Penguin, Harmondsworth, 1975pb
Concise, helpful, very readable; no colour but excellent value

Typographic design

Evans H
■ ■ *Editing and design: a five-volume manual of English, typography and layout*
Heinemann, London, 1972–76
How come this journalist fella knows more about typographic design than most designers?

Gill E
■ *An essay on typography*
Sheed and Ward, London, 1931
Get hold of facsimile copy if you can; virtue of this brilliant, quirky piece is as much in its appearance as what it says

Hurlburt A
■ *Layout: the design of the printed page*
Watson-Guptill, New York, 1977
Long-time art director of late lamented *Look* magazine knows what he's talking about

Jaspert W P, Berry W T and Johnson A F
■ ■ ■ *The encyclopaedia of type faces*
Blandford Press, London, 1970
No typographic designer is considered properly equipped unless possessing this book; if you can't afford to buy it, borrow it on indefinite loan, but *get* it

Jennett S
■ ■ ■ *The making of books*
Faber and Faber, London, 1973
Outstanding work, comprehensive but not in any way hard to absorb; strongly recommended

Williamson H
■ ■ ■ *Methods of book design*
Oxford University Press 1966 (new edition due)
Sound, reliable and authoritative; more factual than Jennett but not so lively

Warning: there are dozens, perhaps hundreds, of books on typographic design; most of them are not worth the paper they're written on

Print production and technology

Craig J
- ■ ■ ■ *Production for the graphic designer*
Watson-Guptill, New York/Pitman, London, 1974
Very thoroughly researched, clearly and crisply written, splendidly
illustrated, best in its field by far; unreservedly recommended

- ■ ■ *BS 2961: Typeface nomenclature and classification*
British Standards Institution, London, 1967
One of several attempts at typeface classification; not perfect but
best so far

Hostettler R
- ■ ■ *The printer's terms*
SGM, St Gallen/Redman, London, 1959 (new edition due)
Expensive little book but very useful, having more hard facts per
square centimetre than you would have thought possible; impeccably
laid out

Copy editing and proof reading

Butcher J
- ■ ■ *Copy-editing*
Cambridge University Press, 1975
Comprehensive manual, intended for use by subeditors but also
required reading for typographic designers

- ■ ■ ■ *Hart's rules for compositors and readers*
Oxford University Press, 1978
First published in 1893 and now in its thirty-eighth edition;
marvellous little book which is prized possession of every author,
editor, printer and designer who has sense enough to own one

- ■ ■ ■ *BS 5261: Copy preparation and proof correction*
*Part 1: Recommendations for preparation of typescript copy for
printing*
*Part 2: Specification for typographic requirements, marks for copy
preparation and proof correction, proofing procedure*
British Standards Institution, London, 1975 (Part 1) and 1976 (Part
2)
Well-meant attempt to get everyone into line, not without faults
but indispensable nevertheless; hideously expensive, so borrow
someone else's and copy them out

Maps and diagrams

Lockwood A
■ ■ *Diagrams: a visual survey of graphs, maps, charts and diagrams*
Studio Vista, London, 1969
No theory, not much general principle but good collection of
illustrations, sensibly grouped

Monkhouse F J and Wilkinson H R
■ ■ ■ *Maps and diagrams*
Methuen, London, 1971pb
Absolutely first rate treatment; highly recommended to anyone
working in this field or hoping to

Computer usage and data processing

Hollingdale S H and Tootill G C
■ ■ ■ *Electronic computers*
Penguin, Harmondsworth, 1970pb
Layman's guide to Them; surprisingly easy read, so get stuck in

Woolridge S
■ ■ ■ *Data processing made simple*
W H Allen, London, 1976pb
Indispensable if you don't want to look a total thicko when those
data merchants come at you with the jargon

Communication studies, visual perception, semiotics

Bodmer F
■ *The loom of language*
Allen and Unwin, London 1943
You'll need to take this in small instalments over about ten years,
so make sure your local library has one available on demand

Cherry C
■ ■ ■ *On human communication*
Massachusetts Institute of Technology, 1978
Astonishing tapestry, woven from more threads of knowledge than
author's peers thought right or proper when it first appeared in late
fifties, now accepted by all as classic as well as pace-setter

Gregory R L

■ ■ ■ *Eye and brain: the psychology of seeing*
Weidenfeld and Nicolson, London, 1977pb
If you haven't got this book, run – don't walk – and get it today:
you can't afford to miss out on it one more day

Miller G A

■ *The psychology of communication*
Penguin, Harmondsworth, 1968pb
Seven lively essays by eminent psychologist who never pulls rank
on his reader; includes his famous 'Magical number seven, plus or
minus two' which is just up our street

Specially recommended but unclassifiable

Papanek V J

■ ■ ■ *Design for the real world*
Granada, London, 1974pb
Vivid polemical counterblast to glamorous, brittle world of phoney
design, somewhat self-righteous but relieved by warmth and
humour; strongly recommended

Brand S (ed)

■ ■ ■ *The last whole earth catalog: access to tools*
Portola Institute, San Francisco/Penguin, Harmondsworth, 1971 pb
Glorious ragbag of hard information, philosophy, opinion and
poetry, masquerading as iist of goods available; intended as last of
series that began in 1968 but already succeeded by at least one
Epilog, this giant (365 × 275mm) paperback is finest memorial to
California's 'flower power' movement (Peace and Love to you,
Stuart Brand, wherever you are)

Macdonald-Ross M and Smith E

■ ■ ■ *Graphics in text: a bibliography*
Open University, Milton Keynes, 1977
Nearest book to hand in this designer's bookshelf; heartfelt vote of
thanks to authors and to OU's Institute of Educational Technology
for this great boon – you'd be daft not to get hold of one yourself

Pirsig R M

■ ■ ■ *Zen and the art of motor cycle maintenance*
Corgi, London, 1976pb
Is this philosophy, mysticism, whodunnit, travelogue, or extended
love poem to motor cycle: why not get your own copy and find out?